Mo scéal féin, scéal gach duine.

My own story, everyone's story.

What people are saying about *Crafted By Heart*

'In a world that so often measures worth by metrics, outcomes, and the relentless pursuit of performance, this book stands as a luminous act of rebellion. It is a book that dares to place soul before strategy, and heart before hierarchy. Zoë Holland MBE has crafted a work that is not only countercultural, but profoundly ahead of its time, a gentle yet fierce invitation to reclaim the essence of leadership as a deeply human, spiritual, and creative act.

What strikes me most is the courage with which Zoë Holland writes. She weaves together stories of women who have led not from the boardroom, but from the hearth; not with titles, but with grace, compassion, and care. Her words remind us that true leadership is found in the everyday moments of humanity, in the quiet acts of kindness, and in the tending of the inner flame.

This book is a celebration of the soul and of the creative spark that lives within each of us. It is a call to nourish ourselves and others, to honour joy as a lifeline, and to lead with presence and purpose. Zoë Holland MBE challenges the dominant narrative that equates success with sacrifice, and instead offers a vision of leadership rooted in authenticity, connection, and the courage to say a sacred 'no' to systems that ask us to burn out our brilliance just to belong.

As someone who has dedicated my life to pioneering change leadership and championing gender equality, I recognise in this book a kindred spirit. Zoë Holland MBE is a modern Bridget, a flame-keeper, a well-tender, and a visionary who invites us to lead with soul and to create spaces where others can flourish. Her writing is both a sanctuary and a spark, offering daily nourishment and creative inspiration for all who seek to lead differently.

I wholeheartedly endorse Zoë Holland MBE for her boldness, her wisdom, and her unwavering commitment to restoring soul and spirit to the heart of leadership. May this book reach all those who are ready to rise not just with data, but with depth; not just with metrics, but with meaning'.

—**DR. SAM COLLINS**, Founder of Aspire,
www.aspirecompanies.com | *www.drsamcollins.com*

'Zoë Holland invites women (and those who love them) to consider the flames ever-burning in their hearts, to invoke St. Brigid's blessings, to bring their soul-filled selves to leadership. She's woven story, poetry, and practical reflections to guide your journey to deeper, more fulfilling relationships with your work and yourself, and, perhaps most importantly, for you to lead the way to a different sort of future'.

—**LIBBY WAGNER**, Poet, Author, Speaker.
www.libbywagner.com

'This is more than a book; it is a warm invitation to return to what makes us feel alive. Through courage, creativity, and quiet leadership, it reminds us that tending our inner flame is how we light the way for others'.

—**MOLLY HARVEY, FRSA.**, Author, International Speaker,
Transformational Leadership Coach. *www.mollyharvey.com*

'If you're looking for insight, inspiration and practical strategies in becoming a more fulfilled human being and a braver, bolder and more authentic leader then this is a must read. It's an exquisite blend of the sacred and secular weaving ancient inspiration with everyday stories of courage, compassion and bravery most especially when we feel anything but brave. It also offers beautiful questions to reflect upon. These ponderings so often lead to love in action making a positive difference to self, others and the world'.

—HILARY WILSON, International Leadership Coach, Author, Speaker. *www.hilarywilson.net*

'As I read this book written by Zoë but inspired by so many women who have rediscovered joy and the true meaning of leadership from the soul, I already have a list of women to whom I would like to gift it. And it is this desire to reach out, to connect, to create and build community and to share love that marked the beginning of this journey. I already see this book as my companion and I know that it will bring affirmation and life to so many women who are leading us through dark and turbulent times'.

—JANE GUNN, Global Leader in Mediation, Author, International Speaker. *www.janegunn.co.uk*

'Zoë Holland has written the book so many women have been waiting for — one that bridges leadership and lived humanity in a way that finally makes sense. Her writing feels like being wrapped in a shawl woven from light, truth, and lived experience. Her stories move between poetry and practicality with effortless grace, speaking to the creative woman, the wounded woman, the healing woman, and the woman still searching for her own voice. She honours ambition without abandoning tenderness and reminds us of what we already know in our bones: real leadership is born from presence, compassion, and courage. Every woman leading or managing a team, a family, or simply her own life will recognise herself in these pages'.

— **SANDIE SEDGBEER**, Author, Publishing Consultant, Talk TV/ Podcast Host, and Founder of The NO BS Spiritual Book Club. *www.thenobsspiritualbookclub.com*

'Zoë shows us that true leadership begins where courage, compassion, and presence meet. With Brigid's quiet flame woven through her words, *Crafted by Heart* becomes a powerful reminder that soul-led leadership isn't abstract — it's ignited through kindness, joy, and the choices we make every day'.

— **OLIVIA STEFANINO**, Author, Speaker and Creator of 'Unlock Your Money Code'. *www.oliviastefanino.com*

'Zoë Holland's pairing of Creativity and the ancient goddess/ saint Brigid is what drew me to this expansive & practical book. I've studied these topics for decades and was intrigued. As I dove into her simple exercises and savoured her evocative poems, I could sense Zoë's deeply embodied, modern approach to being a leader. Her gentle way of inspiring others to follow their hearts, make beauty with their hands and live more creatively while (re) connecting with Source and specifically, the unique energy which we experience as Brigid, is a gift to all — one that we can enjoy & intentionally practice—anywhere, anytime & with anyone'.

— **ELIZABETH DES ROCHES**, Creatrix. *www.ElizabethdesRoches.com* | *creatrixexperience.substack.com*

CRAFTED BY HEART

Living and Leading with Love

Zoë Holland MBE

This is a thank you.

To every woman who supported Silk Elephant.

To every person who gave, shared,

created, and cared.

And in memory of a remarkable man,

my father,

David Nichols

(7.12.46 — 12.12.2019)

ISBN 978-1-919480-40-4 (print)
ISBN 978-1-919480-41-1 (ebook)

Edited by Sandie Sedgbeer
Photos by Julia Harris, Zoë Holland MBE
Text design and layout by Damian Keenan

This book was typeset in Adobe Garamond Pro, with ITC Century Std Book Cond, Calluna Sans, Clarendon and Cal Uncial used as a display typefaces.

LOVE | LEAD | LIVE | PRESS
www.zoehollandmbe.com

Contents

Brigid, Noble Spirit

The Bridge of Living Flame — From Godess to Saint to Modern Woman

• • • • •

Brigid's legacy carries forward into women rising in today's world. Whether we follow her legend as a woman and Goddess Brigit, or trace her historical stories as Saint Brigid, she embodies the beauty found in women. She is an archetype of rich diversity; a torchbearer who keeps the creative light alive through nature, poetry and art, and a healer who mends what is broken. The common thread through all her stories is transformation, like a flame that changes everything it touches.

Transformation has been part of her story, even from the evolution from Goddess to Saint when Christianity took root in Ireland. Saint Brigid of Kildare inherited much of the sacred territory from her mythological roots, becoming a patroness of learning and craft, of compassion and fire.

Her name has travelled through Irish history. *Brigit* in Old Irish, *Brighid* in later forms, *Brigida* in Latin, and *Bridget* in English - all from the root 'brig'; 'high,' 'noble,' 'exalted.'

Many today know her simply as *Brigid*, and that is the form that feels closest to her spirit for me — though it is *Bridget* I turn to as a modern incarnation of all her wonder and diversity.

I see Bridget as more than a name; she is a living bridge connecting the past to the present, much like a flame passed hand-to-hand. This living flame carries Brigid's ancient spirit into the lives of women today.

Original painting courtesy of artist Lia Laimböck,
www.lialaimbock.com

This light at the heart of modern Bridgets unites the beautiful women I know; women who lead and live life with love. I imagine her spirit walking beside them. This same spirit inspired the women who lovingly crafted hearts for my charity, weaving compassion from their own hearts. In this modern form, her spirit kindled a global movement of handmade love.

I am gently reminded of the imaginary Bridget my daughter and I encountered at the cinema earlier this year. The Bridget that drew us into joyful dialogue about the beauty of imperfection and the quiet grace of being deeply self-aware. That conversation opened tender truth; beauty can be messy, complicated, and gloriously non-conforming.

This Bridget, modern and ordinary, stands at a threshold—a metaphorical doorway between the sacred and everyday life, between imagination and reality. She becomes an icon, a goddess of the in-between, appearing whenever another woman lights a fire for creativity, love, and the wonder of what it is to be messily human.

I invite women to rise with the light of Brigid's living flame in a way that speaks to now; by walking the path of life and leadership as Bridgets. Women who transform. Women who love. Women who heal. Women who walk the path of the soul.

Welcome

By Donna Ashworth

Welcome to this book and all the love it has to offer to all the women before, to all the women of today and all the women who are yet to come.

Zoe is a true visionary, with feet firmly on ancient and intuitive soil. She is a fire starter in the most healing of ways.

My poem *The Women Before* is gifted to this book.

Photo by Julie Harris

Handmade hearts from *Silk Elephant* — love, transmuted by women's hands

The Women Before

'It is not just your mother who may walk with you in spirit, it is her mother too, and her mother's mother. And her mother's friends, who loved by choice and not blood. And the women before them. Generations and generations of female energy, watching in admiration as you forge ahead with living *better*, feeling *better*, accepting *better*, than they ever did. As they very much hoped you would. So, when you feel low, lonely or unloved, remember them, *feel* them. They are with you, and they burn brightly with their boundless light, in everything you do. You, my friends, are the 'moment in time' of many women gone before, and you will lay pathways, like they did, for those who come up next. What a beautiful, unending legacy'.

—from 'Wild Hope'

A Heart in Her Hands

Opening Reflection

I want to share this photo with you from my father's funeral as an invitation to pause. To reflect. It is an image of love: both given and received. A simple heart, felted and sewn by hand, carrying within it something far greater than fabric and thread.

Behind this heart is a story. A story of the quiet, unstoppable power of women. Of compassion. Of community. Of what it means to lead from the heart; with fire, with tenderness, with hands that both hold and shape.

This book is a tribute to them, the mothers, daughters, sisters, friends—women who may never have worn the title of CEO, but who led in the most powerful ways: with grace, courage, and care. Each brought her own story of struggle and triumph.

I had the privilege of walking alongside them through the founding of our charity, Silk Elephant, during the pandemic years of 2020 to 2022.

Their kindness shaped me.

Their strength moved me.

And their love is stitched into every page of this book.

Because of them, I am a better mother, wife, friend, and colleague.

Because of them, I understand now that leadership begins not in the spotlight but in the everyday moments of humanity.

They brought me into deep connection with a lineage older than memory: women tending hearths and hopes, crafting warmth from what they had. Women like Brigid—saint and goddess, flame-keeper and well-tender—who stands at the threshold between worlds, drawing to herself those from every faith and none. Brigid, whose story is woven from both Christian and pagan threads, has always gathered women from all walks of life, nourishing them in the liminal spaces where old boundaries dissolve and new belonging is born.

Her legacy is one of embrace. She is the bridge between traditions, the hearth at the centre, the invitation to gather. In her spirit, women have come together, across centuries, cultures, and beliefs, to share, to create, to heal, and to lead with love—just like the women who crafted hearts and other gifts for my charity and helped to distribute them around the world.

I would not be the leader I am today without the threads every woman who supported my charity wove into every handmade heart and gift—threads not unlike the ones Brigid herself might have spun: humble, luminous, enduring.

This is a thank you.

To every woman who supported our movement.

To every person who gave, shared, created, and cared.

Silk Elephant and the love it shared brought me home, to my own heart, and to a deep, soul-level belonging.

May its spirit, and the spirit of Brigid in all her guises, saint and goddess, flame-keeper and bridge-builder, ancient and ever-renewing, reach you, too.

And may you find inspiration in the stories of the women I share in this book; women who gather others at the hearth of compassion, who lead with courage and care, and who weave warmth and hope from the simplest threads. They carry the essence of ancient Brigid into the Bridget of today.

This book is for them, and for you—wherever you are, and whatever story you are weaving next.

Zoë

'Your joy is your sorrow unmasked.
And the selfsame well
from which your laughter rises
was oftentimes filled
with your tears'.

– Kahlil Gibran, The Prophet

Let this be your reminder:

That the soul is not found in perfection,

but in the places where sorrow softened you,

where grief carved space for grace,

and where the shadow became the soil

from which your joy could bloom.

—Zoë

Out of the Shadows and Into the Soul

In February 2020, I took a trip to Delhi, India. My father had passed away just three months earlier, and I was in the raw, uncertain beginning of navigating that loss. I felt adrift, untethered by grief, orphaned by absence. A dark shadow hung over me, and I struggled to find light.

India welcomed me with love.

If you've been to India, you'll understand the aliveness it brings: the ancient architecture, the incessant symphony of honking horns, the humid heat, the vibrant colours, the multitude of smells — every sense is awakened. It's a place where you can't escape the pulse of life.

Two days after arriving in Delhi, I visited the Gurdwara Bangla Sahib, a magnificent Sikh temple devoted to service. There, I learned that the community feeds an extraordinary 30,000 to 40,000 people a day for free, nourishing those living in poverty. The temple hums with compassion. Amid the heat and crowds, there is a remarkable stillness. A silent invitation to simply be.

I sat cross-legged in the heat, and memories of my father and his two-year journey with blood cancer rose gently to the surface. What came wasn't just pain — but warmth. The kindness that had held my family through that time: the soup left on doorsteps, the groceries delivered without a word, the hugs in coffee shops. But the moment that lived most vividly in my heart was one of pure, wordless connection between strangers.

I was making tea in the family room on the Palatine Ward at The Christie Hospital, just after we'd been told that my father's condition was terminal. As I stood in silence, stunned by the words *'It's just a matter of time,'* a young woman named Katie quietly reached out and placed a handmade heart in my hand. She said nothing.

But her gesture spoke volumes:

I see you. I've got you. I care.

A moment silent of sound yet deafening with love. A gift given in compassion. That single, quiet act planted a seed in me.

Brigid

Perhaps it was Brigid—saint of the hearth and goddess of the flame—who stood silently beside me that day, planting the seed of soul-led leadership. She walks between worlds, tending sorrow with compassion and weaving light from silence. In every act of kindness, she rises.

A Vision

That seed planted in me at Gurdwara, became a vision: to create a charity devoted to small, meaningful acts of kindness—one gift, one heart at a time. A week after returning from India, as the world braced for the pandemic, I sat at my kitchen table with four friends and a blank sheet of paper. An hour later, Silk Elephant was born.

In just four months, we grew from five women to a network

of over 700 creative volunteers — sewing, crafting, and hand-making hearts and gifts. Supported by eight incredible kindness ambassadors across the UK, we began to distribute these hearts to hospitals, care homes, and communities in need.

By the end of the pandemic, we had delivered over 110,000 handmade gifts across the UK, Europe, the US, and India. But the numbers, while powerful, were never the point. What mattered most was the energy woven into each offering: woman to woman, heart to heart. The fierce, quiet power of collective compassion.

Now, when I think about every handmade heart and gift, I feel the spark of Brigid's fire and a drop from her well. The charity's gifts lit the way through the dark period of COVID. As women, we gathered to tend the world with love.

Brigid's presence is felt wherever women gather to tend sorrow with love, to transform grief into hope, to create warmth from what they have. I believe her spirit is alive in every act of compassion, in every circle of hands that craft, comfort, and heal. The flame and the well, one offering light, the other sustenance, remind us that leadership is both about kindling possibility and about holding space for restoration.

It is this spirit — ancient and ever-renewing — that was kindled through Silk Elephant.

The women who gathered to tend with love redefined everything I believed about leadership.

Leadership isn't about hierarchy or ego. It's not about having all the answers.

It begins humbly, humanly, and compassionately, with the courage to act.

It's not a destination, it's a becoming.

It's not strategy, it's soul.

This book is my offering

Seven invitations to ground you when you feel uncertain, inspire you when you're empty, connect you when you feel alone, and nourish you when you can't breathe from the madness.

This is an invitation to walk with me, and to sing to the part of you that wants to lead from presence. May the spirit of Brigid—flame and well, ancient and modern—walk with us, wherever we gather to tend the world with love.

Let us rise with Brigid's spirit and become the modern Bridgets who lead with grace.

Zoë at the Kildare Mural — created by Mister Copy as part of the Brigid 1500 celebrations, 2024

Invocation of Brigid

'She who walks between worlds—
Saint of the hearth, goddess of the flame,
keeper of wells and weaver of light.
In sorrow, she tends.
In silence, she listens.
In every act of compassion, she rises.
Let her presence be felt in our hands,
in our hearts,
and in the soul of our leadership'.

—Zoë

1

Feed the Soul

Bia Anama*

* The Irish phrase for **'food of the soul'** is **'Bia Anama'** (pronounced *bee-ah AH-nuh-ma*). It combines **'bia'** *(food)* and **'anam'** *(soul)*, creating a poetic expression of nourishment beyond the physical. In Irish tradition, the soul is often spoken of in blessings and prayers, and this phrase evokes the idea of feeding the spirit with care, beauty, and presence.

Feed the Soul

Leadership begins from within.

Tend your inner flame.

Reclaim your passion and purpose.

Before we lead others,

we must nourish ourselves

and kindle the joy of imagination.

This is the foundation—

soul before strategy.

Soul

'Soul—the quiet, indefinable glow—
where we meet ourselves whole,
and enter the dance
between spirit and being.
When we feed our soul,
we begin to sing the meaning of life
echoing the song of being.
From here, the world blooms in glorious technicolour,
and we walk its landscape
with awe and grace'.

—Zoë

The First Flame - A Seed of Soul

My charity, Silk Elephant, began not with a plan, but with a feeling. That moment in the Gurdwara Temple, where the living memory of human connection through a gift given in silence, was a feeling of coming home that I wanted others to experience. I didn't know it then, but that moment—the simplicity of it, the quiet courage of it—was the first flame.

When I returned home from India, there was no five-year strategy, no thoughts around a glossy launch, and no desire to draft a polished pitch document. The planning started with just four women sitting around my kitchen table, hearts open, hands empty, and a blank sheet of paper between us. The world outside was beginning to go into lockdown; a connected, fast-paced world was shutting down. But in my kitchen, we paused as something ancient and alive began to rise.

The days that followed moved like wildfire. Ideas became action. Words became stitches into handmade hearts. Grief became creation and love shared in simplicity. Within several weeks, Silk Elephant was no longer just an idea—it was a living, breathing community of over 700 volunteers. It became a kindness movement rooted not in hierarchy or corporate strategy, but in heart and in the quiet beauty of love made visible.

I look back at that first flame and think about the purity and rawness of what started such a beautiful journey. How something so simple could start something so lasting. My purpose was born of surrender to that deep internal voice that wanted to share that moment of remembrance in Gurdwara.

When I think of those early days, I think of Brigid, the way she kindled her own flame, with small acts of courage and compassion. Like Brigid, who gathered women around her hearth and wove community from the simplest threads, we, too, began with nothing but open hearts and a willingness to serve. The first flame was a living invitation to create warmth, to offer sanctuary, to let love be the spark that lights the way.

We all have moments like this — times when we touch something deep within us. An inner voice guiding us to where we belong. This is what shapes our purpose. This is where our values are born. And the closer we live and work in alignment with those values, the more we listen to that inner voice, the more soulfully we lead.

REFLECTION

- Brigid's flame was kindled in the quiet. In the small acts of courage that became community.
- What is the first flame you remember?
- A moment when something stirred within you—quiet but insistent. What would it mean to honour that spark today?
- Before you read on, take a quiet minute to ground.

Tending The Flame

Returning to Now

Pause for a moment and notice your breath.

Let it draw you back from the noise of

thought into the quiet rhythm of being.

Presence doesn't ask you to do anything—

it simply invites you to arrive.

As you breathe, feel the small,

steady flame of awareness within you.

Tend it with attention; let it remind you that

every new beginning starts here.

Soul Before Strategy

The charity ignited the kind of energy that can't be manufactured or measured. It was the kind that vibrates beneath the surface when you are doing the things you were born to do. A silent whisper of love and doing something that makes you feel whole. It came from deep within — from a place where purpose meets presence, and passion becomes service. It was as if, for the first time, all of me had come into alignment: my values, my experience, my voice, my community, my longing to give and love. Out of the shadow of grief, a seed of joy began to germinate.

The charity didn't just nourish me; it nourished others. What fuelled all those women who supported the charity wasn't the idea of reward or success. It was soul.

People chose to help because they felt inspired. Many of our volunteers were elderly women, living alone, who found not only a creative outlet in the charity but also a sense of connection and purpose. It created a supportive community and a meaningful way to give. I received countless letters from volunteers who said that being part of Silk Elephant brought them hope and joy. There was as much gratitude in giving as in receiving a handmade heart.

What we were creating was a circle of love born from the simplest acts of kindness and the humblest materials: scraps of fabric, leftover wool, and the final thread from an embroidery reel. It was raw and honest. That was the beauty. Hands gathering imperfection into love.

We also welcomed young teenagers who felt disconnected from friends and school. They, too, felt seen. They felt useful. They felt part of something that mattered. That's what feeding the soul does — it invites others to remember their own. We weren't just crafting hearts; we were remembering ours.

The charity gave me the wisdom to understand that when the soul is stirred, it speaks in the language of generosity. That language unfolded not just in my kitchen, but in living rooms, sewing rooms, and spare bedrooms across the country. The flame caught elsewhere, often in the quietest, most unexpected corners.

Lorraine Waugh and Jackie Dean were two such sparks. We'd never met before. They found us through a simple Facebook post and reached out with a question: *How can we help?*

At the time, they were already sewing scrubs for frontline workers in Scottish hospitals. They had made thousands and distributed them. On our first Zoom call, what struck me the most wasn't their success and skill — it was their *soulful sincerity.* Here were two women, sitting at home in the middle of a global crisis, not overwhelmed by it, but *ignited* by a sense of shared humanity.

There was no performance, no pretence. Just purpose. And a powerful desire to give.

Lorraine and Jackie quickly became our Scottish Kindness Ambassadors. But the title was never the point — it simply named what was already true. They became the beating heart of a kindness production line that rippled from the Scottish mainland to the Outer Hebrides.

Together with a team of Scottish volunteers, they stitched tartan hearts — each one infused with Scottish spirit and stitched with love. These were sacred hearts.

Other Kindness Ambassadors joined the charity from around the county — Julie White, Helen Selwood, Kay Lee, Jo Deighton, Jayne Burnham, Wendy Parker and Ros Hammond. What these women created wasn't just a supply chain — it was a soul chain, an *Aon Cri*, a web of connection, compassion, and creative action. Thousands of hearts passed through many hands, many homes, care homes, hospitals and hospices. They travelled far, but their message was always the same:

You are not alone.

You are seen.

You are held.

*You are **loved**.*

Our volunteers' devotion lit up every space they touched. Communities began to knit themselves together again, not through ambition and fanfare, but through care. And in witnessing their fire, my own grew stronger.

This is what feeding the soul does. It spreads. It never stays contained because soul, when awakened, becomes contagious.

'The soul of a leader is a beautiful landscape
to be walked with grace
and honoured with reverence'.

—Zoë

In the traditional language of leadership, we're taught to start with structure—strategy, systems, performance, outcomes, profit and loss. But in my experience, the most powerful business ideas don't begin with a PowerPoint presentation. They begin with a spark. *Silk Elephant* was never born from a business plan. It was born from a question: *What can love do?* And that's what made it thrive.

Today, successful businesses start with a purpose-led vision. Fletchers Group, where I serve as CCO, began over 20 years ago with a simple question: **How can we help injured people?** This remains at the core of our business. Even in the boardroom, our first act is not numbers but presence: remembering why we are here — to restore lives and protect dignity. That reminder is our flame. It sets the stage for everything we do, shaping and guiding every level of leadership

When we lead from the soul, we access something beyond motivation. We tap into *meaning* — that deep, internal alignment where who we are and what we do comes into resonance. It's not about ego, status, or external validation. It's about truth. Integrity. Heart. In great businesses and organisations, strategy is important — but it should follow soul, not replace it. When we lead with soul, the strategy becomes clearer. The right people arrive. The path opens. Not always easily, but *honestly*.

The modern workplace often celebrates performance at the expense of purpose. We are trained to look outward for direction — metrics, goals, benchmarks — while our inner compass grows quiet. Yet, time and again, research quietly affirms what many of us feel in our bones: People do their best work when they feel connected to something greater than themselves.

When I witnessed women like Lorraine and Jackie come alive through service, I saw what happens when strategy bows to soul. They weren't waiting to be told what to do — they already knew. Their clarity didn't come from a job description. It came from within.

That is the power of soul-led leadership. It doesn't command — it *calls*. It invites. It awakens.

Have you noticed how it feels to be in the room with a leader leading from soul?

There is so much energy that comes with them. They fill the room with a pulse and vibrancy that's felt. I recall this vividly, from meeting Dr Sam Collins for the first time in Manchester at one of her APSPIRE conferences. Sam is a female activist, changing the world for women and girls, and helping other women do the same. When Sam stood at the lectern, she shone. She spoke from a deep knowing of someone who is whole and alive. She held the room with grace and fun! She is a modern Bridget. She spoke with reverence and honesty, whilst sharing the problems with her pop-socks and menopausal sweats. She sings the meaning of life. There is a reason the late Queen Elizabeth II named her one of the UK's most influential women. She is a soul powerhouse!

When we lead with passion and purpose like Sam, we're not just managing projects and delivering profit and/or results—we're creating meaning. We are stewards of energy and protectors of purpose. We become evangelists for all those around us. When we turn away from the grey corporate landscape of chasing success and wooing ego, our shared landscape becomes alive with colour and an abundance of shades of green.

I often talk about leadership as a privilege and the responsibilities that come with it. To lead with soul is not indulgence. It is an honoured responsibility. It is saying, 'I will not pour from an empty vessel that I have not first filled'. Saint Brigid would have known this. Her leadership began with the tending of the flame and the field, the offering of bread, the giving of shelter, and the deep listening that restores dignity to the unheard.

REFLECTION

- What will you do with this one extraordinary life you've been given?

Daily Nourishment

'Tending the soul begins with daily nourishment– through warmth, wonder, and quiet rituals that restore us to ourselves'.

—Zoë

Saint Brigid of Kildare knew this well. Her leadership was not forged in grand gestures, but in the humble acts of care, baking bread, weaving cloth, lighting the hearth. She understood that nourishment is sacred—that tending the flame within requires the body, the heart and the spirit.

As *Silk Elephant* grew, there were late nights, endless packages arriving, trips to the post office and moments of exhaustion. What kept me going were the small, luminous gifts of daily life: handwritten letters of thanks arriving quietly in the post, the squeals of my rare breed pigs, Winne and Ginnie, as I arrived on the local farm where they were kept, the walks in nature, and the joy of baking cakes together with my kids—licking the buttercream from the bowl, smiling over perfect sponges and sharing stories of memories of Dad.

These moments were not distractions from my leadership— they defined it. They reminded me that small daily moments bring us into presence. We lead best when we are fed by love, lit by purpose and held by ritual.

In our modernity of busyness, action, and the juggle of life and work, daily nourishment of the soul is a necessity. It is how we refill the vessel from which we pour. For *modern Bridgets,* it is the welcoming of the buttercream joy, the handwritten grace, the sacred pause between the doing. It is where soul meets simplicity—before strategy. Leading the charity was where I drew my strength. Just as Brigid tended the hearth and heart, I learnt to tend my own—daily, gently, and with love.

REFLECTION Nourishing your soul

- What daily rituals nourish your soul?
- Where in your life do you feel most aligned with your values?

Letting in Joy – The Quiet Rebellion of Delight

Joy is a lifeline to the soul. Yet in the relentless cadence of leadership, joy is often the first thing we trade. Then, when joy leaves, something vital goes with it—the spark that makes us human, the energy that makes us whole.

I saw this truth vividly in a coaching session with a senior leader. She was navigating menopause, working long hours in a demanding corporate role, and trying to energise her peer group to create new operational solutions. When she arrived, her energy was flat. I felt the weight of her exhaustion and a quiet sadness beneath the surface.

I asked gently: *'What have you lost?'*

Her answer came without hesitation: *'I've lost joy'.*

Amid striving, she had lost her sense of fun. When we explored the last time she felt truly alive, her face lit up: *'My last drumming gig'.* Here was a woman in her fifties who had played in a band in her youth—and still loved to drum when life allowed. The sadness was that she had stopped, letting work and life crowd out her joy.

As we talked, it became clear that her struggle to motivate her peers wasn't about strategy—it was about energy. Without her own joy, others couldn't follow.

Sometimes, feeding the soul is about a quiet rebellion—a refusal to let busyness steal what makes us feel alive. It's about becoming a joy activist: putting joy at the centre, creating moments of delight both in and out of work.

She made a commitment that day. A few weekends later, she returned to her band for a drumming session and invited her peer group to a karaoke night. Joy began to ripple outward. Her energy shifted. Her leadership blossomed. And her team responded.

When we become joy activists, we spark something contagious. We invite others into the celebration. We role model fun and laughter and keep the flame alive.

Brigid knew this well. Her flame was for warmth and celebration. She wove joy into the ordinary: baking bread, tending the hearth, gathering women in laughter and song. Joy was her leadership language. It is ours too, if we choose it.

When we let joy in, we lead differently. We giggle. We laugh. We listen. We create. We become leaders who ignite possibility and creativity. Joy is contagious. It ripples through teams, cultures, and communities. It reminds us that leadership is just as much about aliveness as it is outcomes.

REFLECTION **Joy**

- Where in your life have you silenced joy for the sake of duty?
- What small act of delight could you welcome today?
- How might joy become a leadership practice—not an afterthought, but a way of being?

PRACTICE Letting In Joy

- **Joy Rituals:** Begin the day with something that makes you smile—a walk, a song, a cup of tea in your favourite mug, a splash of colour.
- **Joy Activation Slips:** Write yourself a note that says, *Joy matters. I matter.* Keep it where you can see it.
- **Team/Family Invitations:** Ask your team/family, *What brings you joy? How can we make space for that here?*
- **Threshold Moments:** Pause before meetings. Take one deep breath. Ask: *What would it feel like to lead from joy?*
- **Affirmation:** Put your hand on your heart and say out loud or in your mind: *'I am joy. Joy is within me'.*

When We Lose the Flame

If soul-led leadership is about presence and purpose in life and in work, then its opposite is something many of us have witnessed or been part of. For me, it took the shape of a Dictaphone in the early part of my career. It began on a day I asked to leave work early to attend my son's sports day. I had been working long hours for weeks in the lead up to a preliminary trial on a child brain injury case. I had already missed the school summer fair due to work. It was a simple, human request—a mother wanting to show up, wanting to take part in the joy of sports day and show my son that I cared about his egg-and-spoon race.

But the response I received wasn't one of empathy or understanding. Instead, my senior leader leaned back in her chair and smiled with a kind of steely pride. She told me how, during the birth of her first child, she had dictated work emails and memos from her hospital bed—*on the way into the delivery room*. She shared the story as if it were a trophy. A mark of dedication. She talked about the need to consider my career path, what was expected of a female partner in a law firm, and what she had sacrificed to live in her beautiful home in Wilmslow. Something I, too, should aspire to.

But I didn't feel inspired. I felt something else entirely: *resistance and sadness.* I nodded politely. I said thank you. And then I quietly packed my bag and walked out of the office. I went to my son's sports day. It may seem like a small act, but in that moment, it was everything. It was a quiet rebellion. A sacred *no* to a system that had long asked women to burn out their brilliance just to be allowed to belong. I felt sadness for her. Her focus on productivity and her career had turned one of life's most precious moments — giving birth — into another bullet point on the daily agenda, and another step up the corporate ladder. On my son's sports day, I met my own Gollum — not in her, but in the shadow of what I feared I might become if I kept trading my soul for status.

I have carried the memory and feeling from that day with me ever since.

Each compromise, each silence, each dismissal of what truly matters begins to dim the flame, and if we are not careful — if we do not protect that flame — it flickers. It vanishes. And one day we wake up not knowing who we've become. This is why *feeding the soul* isn't self-indulgent. It's a radical act of remembrance. It's leadership that chooses life over performance as the measure of success.

In choosing presence over performance, I honoured the flame. A quiet act of soulful leadership. One that Brigid might have recognised. We cannot lead from the soul and craft with the heart if we are starving for meaning, in and out of work. We must feed the flame, not with sacrifice but with sacred choices.

Over the past three years in my coaching practice, I've met many women who walk with their own Gollum, an inner shadow that whispers doubt, steals joy, and dims the flame. One such woman was a board-level leader at Google. When I first learned of her global role, I felt a wobble of inadequacy, wondering how I could possibly be of value to someone whose career shone so brightly on the world stage.

But what unfolded in our first session surprised me. It was early December, a time when many are preparing for the holidays. I opened with a simple question: '*What would you like to focus on today?*' Without hesitation, she replied, '*I want to be present with my children while they open their Christmas gifts*'.

Her words landed with quiet weight. She spoke of how work had become so all-consuming that she couldn't remember a Christmas morning spent fully in the moment. Her mind was always elsewhere: on emails, on tidying the wrapping paper, on preparing dinner, on the endless tasks that filled the day. What she longed for was simple: to sit with her children, to see their faces light up, to feel the joy of presence.

As she wept, we gently walked through the steps together: how to close the laptop, switch off the phone, and release the mental clutter that had taken root. I held the space as a witness to her longing. A mother's love aching to be felt more fully.

At the end of the session, she smiled through tears and offered two words: '*Thank you*'. In that moment, I understood my role— not to fix, but to hold love. To help her find her way back to the quiet joy of being present. And in doing so, to feed her soul—and the souls of those she loved most.

REFLECTION Protecting the Flame

- Even the eternal flame must be tended. Brigid's fire was kept alive by many hands.
- When your own light flickers, who or what helps you remember?
- What sacred 'no' might you need to say, to protect your sacred 'yes'?

Feeding The Soul of Others – The Privilege of Leadership

Leadership, to me, is a privilege. Whether in the boardroom, in a charity, at home, or in the quiet moments with friends, leadership is the sacred act of tending to the souls of others. It is about presence.

When I speak of feeding the soul, I mean the kind of leadership that listens beyond the surface and remains curious about where someone is truly at, not just in their work, but in their life. It's about asking not just *'How are you?'* but *'How are you in the wholeness of who you are'?*

In my own leadership practice, this shows up in how I conduct performance and development reviews. I always begin with what I call a 'welfare check-in'. I leave the formality behind and take this as a moment of genuine care. I ask, *'How are you?'* and I mean it. I listen not just with my ears, but with my heart. I want to know what's stirring beneath the surface, what's bringing someone joy, what's weighing them down, what they're longing for, and what they need to feel whole.

This kind of leadership is sacred.

Saint Brigid of Kildare is the living ember at the heart of this tradition. As Nancy Fitzgerald writes in *Brigid's Mantle: Finding the Fiery Saint of Kildare at the Heart of Celtic Spirituality*, Brigid was a woman who fed the soul of her community through acts of fierce compassion and sacred care. Her leadership was a quiet, luminous presence. The monastery at Kildare was more than a place of worship. It was a sanctuary for the soul, a hearth where the stranger was welcomed, the sick were tended, and each person was invited to rekindle their own inner spark.

I have witnessed this same soul-tending in my own journey with Silk Elephant. As the charity unfolded, so, too, did a circle of Kindness Ambassadors; women who listened deeply to their hearts and found their own ways to serve. My role was simply to hold the space and ask, '*What would nourish you?*' And then trust them to follow the thread of their own light.

Each Kindness Ambassador shaped their own creative community. They found ways to distribute hearts and care packages that reflected their own gifts and passions. Wendy Parker, based in Nottingham, created a network through elderly care homes, hospices, and hospitals. She brought her therapy dog, Buttons — a beautiful cockapoo — into those spaces, living her dream of delivering love and joy. Buttons became a messenger of kindness, and Wendy became a flame keeper in her own right.

REFLECTION **Feeding the Soul of Others**

To feed the soul of another is sacred work. Brigid welcomed the stranger, tended the sick, and held space for the spark in every soul. Who are you being called to nourish—not with answers, but with presence?

Modern Bridgets – Feeding The Souls of Others

As modern women, modern Bridgets, we carry Brigid's mantle in many ways. We do it in boardrooms, yes, but also in bedrooms, kitchens, and quiet conversations. We do it when we ask our children what they want to do, what makes them feel alive.

When my eldest son, Elliott, finished his degree in mechanical engineering, he felt a sense of loss. The path he had followed no longer felt like his own. So, I encouraged him to pause. To reflect. To ask himself: '*What will make me feel alive*'?

He chose music. He followed the spark, and I watched him transition from a place of deep depression to a place of joy. He enrolled in a second degree in music production and sound engineering and flourished. He comes alive at his production desk. He returns from the studio with light in his eyes. Now in his third year of a five-year part-time degree, he consistently achieves firsts.

My role wasn't to direct but to hold space, feed the soul, and help him tend the flame.

Brigid teaches us that leadership is about care and avoiding control. It's about helping others find their spark and gently encouraging them to keep it alive. Whether we are leading teams, raising children, or supporting friends, we are invited to be soul tenders. Flame keepers. Modern Bridgets.

When we feed our own souls, we become a wellspring for others. This is Brigid's living legacy to tend the inner flame so that its warmth radiates outward, lighting the way for those around us. I have met many women who embody this spirit, but few shine quite like Nicola Wood, a true modern Bridget.

Nicola's journey began in the shadow of adversity. At just 36, Nicola Wood faced breast cancer while already living with rheumatoid arthritis. In her suffering, she saw the deeper grief of other women losing their hair, and with it, their dignity. Nicola vowed to restore both. From her kitchen table, she built The Wonderful Wig Company, now serving thousands. Yet when she speaks, it isn't of business success but of dignity, beauty, and hope. She is a modern Bridget—fierce, tender, visionary.

REFLECTION

- Brigid's flame was never hers alone. It was a shared fire, passed from hand to hand, heart to heart. You are part of that lineage now.
- Who in your life carries a spark that needs tending?
- How might you hold space—not to fix, but to witness?

* * *

'Be a lamp,
or a lifeboat,
or a ladder.
Help someone's soul heal.
Walk out of your house
Like a shepherd'.

— Rumi

Creativity as Soul Expression

Creativity is one of the soul's languages. Whether we are hand-making crafts, playing, writing, baking, stitching, or dreaming, creative acts bring our imagination to life; they invite our soul's expression and help us remember who we are and what brings us alive.

Brigid, as both saint and goddess, is not only keeper of the flame and the well, but also patron of poets, artists, and smiths. Her spirit reminds us that creativity is not reserved for the gifted few; it is the birthright of all who long to bring something new into the world. Whether we are stitching hearts, baking bread, composing music, or finding new ways to care for others, we are engaging in the sacred work of creation. In times of uncertainty, it is creativity and imagination that transform sorrow into beauty and longing into action. When we feed our souls, we awaken our creative fire, one that lights the way for ourselves and for those we lead. To lead with soul is to honour the creative spark within, and to invite others to do the same.

Creativity is not limited to the arts. It shapes the way we solve problems, nurture relationships, adapt to change, and find joy in the ordinary. It is there when we improvise a meal from what's in the cupboard, invent a new family ritual, or reimagine how we show up at work. Sometimes, it's as simple as baking a cake from scratch, mixing the tastiest butter cream, planting a summer flowerpot and watching it bloom, or picking up a book of poetry and letting the words open something new inside us. Every act of making, imagining, or experimenting is an affirmation of life.

I was once asked to host an afternoon with six senior legal leaders. The energy between them had grown stagnant, and the CEO felt they were lacking a solutions-focused attitude. I decided to step away from PowerPoints. Instead, I asked the team to imagine what their work could feel like if it were fully alive. Most of them just stared at me. One asked, '*What do you mean*'? So, I asked them to remember a favourite childhood memory where they felt nothing but joy. We spread out large sheets of paper, scattered coloured pens, paints, stickers, felt shapes, and magazines across the tables. We gave them permission to play. At first, people hesitated. Some colleagues muttered that they 'weren't creative', and others seemed embarrassed. But within minutes, the room shifted. Laughter and giddiness filled the space, and the stilted conversation began to loosen.

By the end, we had a collective collage of possibilities, images of doors opening, flowers growing, aeroplanes, beaches, forests, a chopper motorbike, racing cars, one large smiling sun and a glowing crescent moon! Imagination was released with a sense of joy. That exercise changed how they saw each other. They began to lead with more openness, honesty, and courage. Creativity had shifted the collective energy, lighting a new fire. When leaders create space for imagination, they build trust, openness, and courage. Creativity is less about the artefacts produced and more about the energy it releases in people.

Leadership research supports this truth. Linda Hill and colleagues, in *Collective Genius*, remind us that the best leaders are not those with all the answers, but those who create environments where imagination and experimentation thrive. Similarly, Otto Scharmer, in *Theory U*, describes leadership as the capacity to sense and actualise emerging future possibilities. Each of these echoes Brigid's gift: the invitation to see beyond what is, to imagine what could be, and to kindle the courage to bring it into being.

The theme of imagination and creativity carries through my

experience. Brigid's patronage of poets reminds me that words can heal, connect, and ignite. After losing my father, I turned to poetry to rekindle the creative part of myself I thought lost. What began as a personal practice in imagination and gratitude became a way to honour the women around me. On International Women's Day, I shared this poem as a tribute to the women who hold, inspire, and walk beside one another.

Head, Heart & Soul

'Together, we share our wisdom,
unfold our journeys,
and trace the road that led us here.
We are a force of intelligent women.
Together, we embody resilience.
We speak with lived intelligence,
and we are empowered.
Together, we sit in the sunshine.
We connect our hearts.
We feel.
We love.
We hold
each other.
Our hearts open wide
and we share our joy.
Together, we connect
with our silent knowing.

Our souls converse,
our spirit as one.
With head, heart, and soul,
we shine with beauty,
we move with grace.
We will always be that way.
Together,
our light shines bright.
Through that light
we hold each other
as we continue our destiny'.

— Zoë

To feed the soul is to create space for a spark. When we allow ourselves and those we lead to experiment, dream, make, and play, we do more than innovate; we remember who we are. Creativity is the beating heart of leadership. It is the fire that keeps us alive. By tending our creative spark, we build the foundation for resilience; each small creative act fuels the fire to face what lies ahead.

One powerful way I've found to feed the soul creatively is through Julia Cameron's 'The Artist's Date' — a weekly ritual of creative replenishment. It is a sacred appointment with yourself, for play, wonder, and joy.

For me, an Artist's Date might be a quiet hour in the second-hand book section of a charity shop, letting poetry find me and then inspire the next poem I am writing. Or a walk through the woods listening to nature, in the rustle of leaves or a gentle breeze. Sometimes it's baking a cake for no reason other than the joy of licking the buttercream from the bowl or visiting an independent gallery and finding a local artist that I have never heard of.

These dates have become an essential part of my weekly routine. And after a full-on week at work, whilst juggling dogs, kids, and visiting mum in a care home, they are moments of sanctuary to rekindle imagination and joy. The Artist's Date is a way of saying: *My soul deserves beauty. Joy matters. I love me.*

It's not always easy to remember this in the busyness of life and the ongoing momentum of daily leadership. When we honour the Artist's Date, we return to our work and our relationships with more presence, more imagination, and more soul.

REFLECTION **Bringing Creativity Into Your Life**

- When was the last time you felt truly creative?
- What small act of making, imagining, or problem-solving brought you alive?
- How might you tend your creative flame today?
- When did you last have an Artist's Date alone?

* * *

'I have been a seeker,
and I still am,
but I stopped asking the
books and the stars.
I started listening
to the teachings
of my own soul'.

– Rumi

'Feed the Soul

Tend the flame within;
let its warmth remind you
that beginnings in quiet
can lead to great things'.

2

Weave Your Tapestry

Fíodóireacht Shaol*

* The Irish phrase for '**weaving of life**' is '**Fíodóireacht Shaol**' (pronounced *FEE-uh-deh-rukht HAY-ol)*. It combines '**fíodóireacht**' *(weaving)* and '**shaol**' *(life)*, creating a poetic expression of existence as an intricate tapestry. In Irish tradition, weaving often symbolizes connection and continuity, and this phrase evokes the idea that every choice, relationship, and moment is a thread in the fabric of life — interlaced with beauty, mystery, and meaning.

Weave a Tapestry

Create a loving community.

Brigid was a weaver of tapestry—not just of cloth but of connection, in the same way woven and hand stitched hearts connected the vulnerable, elderly and sick. This invitation celebrates the act of bringing together community, nurturing relationships, and creating spaces where belonging can bloom.

The Weavers

For the women who stitch soul into their leadership.

'Their hands do not command;
they gather.
Threads of soul, strands of joy,
fibres of energy,
dyed with the colours of courage.
They do not follow the line;
they listen.
To the hush of hearts,
the whisper of belonging,
the pulse of purpose.
They do not weave alone;
they invite.
Each stitch a story,
each knot a knowing,
each patch a prayer.
And what they make is not perfect;
it is whole.
A tapestry of tenderness,
held together
by love'.

—Zoë

Weave a Tapestry

Leadership Through Connection

Opening Reflection – Beyond Running Stitch Leadership

I often speak about what I call *running-stitch leadership*—a term I coined. It's the kind of leadership many of us were shown early on: the leader out front, directing the team from a distance, often working in a silo. It reminds me of my early sewing classes in primary school—in year six, we were each given a small square of Aida cloth, its criss-cross of holes guiding our needles as we learned the running stitch. It was linear. Basic. Functional. A first step as a novice.

In my dusty attic room, tucked inside a box labelled 'Zoë's memory box', lies a patch of fabric bearing my first attempt at the running stitch. Eleven or so straight lines of navy-blue thread stretch across a pale-yellow background, like tiny soldiers marching across the worn gravel of a parade ground. It winks at me, both as a reminder of how much better my sewing is and as a prompt to remind me how far I've come; it's a pause to think about the many threads I've woven through life and leadership to create the rich tapestry I now proudly call my own.

My life's tapestry isn't made of obedient running stitches, neatly following the straight lines of Aida cloth. It's a weave of ups and downs, people and places, tears and laughter—a vibrant, imperfect journey shaped by change and the ebb and flow of everyday experience. At its core are the threads that have always held true: integrity, kindness, and fairness. These are my grounding warp threads; the ones I've carried with me all my life. Then there are those threads that have been in the moment, less predictable, and rich in colour.

My life has been both loom-woven and handmade—and so has my leadership.

On the loom, strong warp threads stretch vertically, giving structure and strength. These are the constants: values, integrity, vision. Into them, the weft threads are woven horizontally, crossing over and under, again and again, building colour, depth, and pattern. These are the relationships, the creativity, the compassion that bring life to the work. Yet not all tapestries are made on looms.

Some are made by hand, improvised, stitched together from scraps and uneven threads. Their beauty lies in their irregularity, in the fingerprints of the maker, in the imperfections that tell stories. Just like the handmade hearts from my charity, crafted during lockdown from whatever our creative volunteers could find at home.

Life and leadership are both like this: part loom, part handmade. They require the strength of structure and the freedom of improvisation. The warp holds us steady; the weft brings us alive. And the handmade parts, the messy, human, imperfect pieces, are often the most meaningful. Great leadership is multi-threaded, multi-textured, alive with connection and choice. It is woven with energy, creating something resilient, radiant, and real.

This is the leadership of modern Bridgets.

Running-stitch leadership shows up when a manager believes they must carry the heavy weight of all the answers, maintain control, and direct from a distance. It's a lonely place, bereft of richness, colour and companionship. It's truly uninspiring. Imagine a headteacher who stands at the front of the assembly, telling children what to do, where to sit, and when to sing. Orderly, yes. Efficient, yes. But it leaves no space for voices to rise in harmonic chorus, or for the energy of the room to joyfully shape the moment. It's leadership in a straight line: safe, contained, lonely and predictable. It doesn't invite connection or creativity. It's a sad and sterile place to be. I have only worked with one such leader. This was the same Gollum who brought the Dictaphone into the delivery room.

By contrast, leadership that weaves a tapestry is more like a primary school art class. I remember in year 6, we gathered as excited children around a shared mural. Our mission was to create an autumn landscape of handprints ready for the Harvest Festival. Each of us brought our giddy hands around the painting table, where a large roll of lining wallpaper lay, inviting us to the fingerpainting party. The outline of the trees and landscape had been pencilled in by our teacher, Miss Forbes; it was for us to create the rest. We were invited to choose one hand or both, or our eager fingertips, and to place them into a variety of child-friendly paint gloop. Can you remember the smell of that paint in school? I remember the whiff of PVA, and it still brings a smile. A scent that called for fun!! And so, with gentle pushing and shoving and a bit of overexuberance, the mural came to life. The result was a bit messy in places, but the harvest landscape was rich and unrecognisable to us. It brought a joining of hands, the dipping of many eager fingertips, and the blending of our creative childhood inspirations. Miss Forbes sat beside us, sometimes reaching over to help and encourage us. She had a wonderful way of inviting the gifts in each of our hands and hearts.

I hear her voice even now, *'Look, Zoë, there is a little space there. How could you make it look like the sun is shining on the trees?'* And so I plonked a hand in bright yellow and blobbed in a glow of sunshine. When I think of a tapestry, that hand blob would be a beautifully woven golden thread of connection, bringing the soul into leadership tapestry. Connection is the thread that binds the tapestry together. Without it, the colours don't meet, and the fabric remains fragile. With it, something strong and beautiful emerges.

REFLECTION Weaving Your Tapestry

- What colour threads do you choose?
- Which colours are missing?
- Where might you create space for voices, perspectives, or talents that are yet to be seen?
- How does running-stitch leadership show up in your life and work?
- What kind of tapestry are you weaving?

Weaving Love – Threads and Flames Across Borders

Brigid was a weaver in every sense, of cloaks, kinship, courage, and she knew the power of weaving deeply. She stitched communities from threadbare beginnings, kindled fires that never went out, and made room at her hearth for every soul, saint or stranger alike.

In the spirit of such weaving, I'm drawn to the rare leadership books that honour connection as craft. Des Dearlove and Lisa

Humphries, in *Connectedness: How the Best Leaders Create Authentic Human Connection in a Disconnected World*, write with a gentle wisdom:

'Connections — building relationships — are intrinsic to good leadership'.

In a delicate way, they bring to life what makes today's leaders true weavers. They celebrate leaders who foster trust, belonging, and authentic human connection through compassion. This is the kind of leadership Brigid modelled — the kind the Brigidine nuns in Kildare have quietly fostered for generations, carrying Brigid's voice and warmth out into the world.

You see it each year during *Féile Bríde*, the festival of St. Brigid, when the Brigidine Sisters open their doors and hearts to pilgrims from every corner. They gather people of all faiths and none, weaving together ritual, poetry, music, and the simple act of sharing bread. In 1993, the Brigidine Sisters rekindled Brigid's sacred flame in Kildare Town, a symbol of hope and hospitality that now burns in the town square — tended by their hand but belonging to all. Through their work at Solas Bhríde, they offer sanctuary, listening, and a sense of belonging to those who seek it, embodying a leadership that is relational, not running stitch, a tapestry of care, not a hierarchy of threads. In their hands, leadership becomes less about position and more about presence — a living, breathing web of kinship, woven anew each day.

'When we put to one side our need to be seen,
we can truly see others and the tapestry starts to live
and breathe, richly, deeply and with reverence'.

— Zoë

In the summer of 2025, I visited Solas Bhríde, Kildare, the home and centre of the last two remaining Brigidine nuns. I was delighted to meet Sister Phil (Philomena) and Sister Rita. I had been guided there by the extraordinary Nóirín Ní Riain — interfaith minister, spiritual singer, and wisdom-keeper whose beautiful singing voice has echoed through Glenstal Abbey and across the world.

The lives of Rita and Phil have been devoted to education, community, and courageous service. Their presence was gentle, yet strong, and deeply grounding. We talked about compassion in leadership. Phil spoke warmly about how when women come together in community, and bring open hearts and minds, compassionate leadership shines, and the breath of unity is softly spoken and woven. It was this gentle collective compassion that enabled Silk Elephant's reach to become global. It was leadership that wove unity amongst communities separated by land and water, religion and culture. And my, how the world needs that right now — in boardrooms, kitchens, and bedrooms alike.

Whilst sitting in the sunshine, we laughed about the 1993 relighting of the Brigid Flame — a moment of renewal in Kildare that, as the sisters told me, apparently set off a fire alarm in a Beijing hotel. (Proof that even sacred flames need risk assessments). That small story carried a bigger truth: the rekindling of Brigid's spirit across the world.

The flame was first re-lit in Kildare's Market Square and has since travelled far, a symbol of peace and presence. The Dalai Lama himself was once welcomed with Brigid's Flame at Solas Bhride, its light offered as a gesture of hope and non-violence. Noirin and I took a moment to reflect by quietly honouring in prayer the proudly displayed photographs of the event. We also took time to gather around the eternal Brigid flame, whilst Noirin sang a deeply moving blessing to Brigid. So many women before me have sat around the flame. A quiet, graceful energy resides there. I carried the essence of that energy home with me, and I feel it with me, as I bring Brigid's spirit into this book. May you imagine the flicker of the flame in your mind's eye and feel it too.

As I gathered my belongings to leave, Sister Rita placed a copy of her book, *Rekindling the Flame*, into my hands. It was a moment of quiet honour — a reminder that the legacy of women who lead with soul is not merely remembered but lived.

Afterwards, I stood beneath the mural of St. Brigid in Kildare town, and I found myself reflecting on the values she embodied: compassion, generosity, courage, and inclusivity.

These aren't just spiritual ideals — they're leadership essentials.

Brigid's spirit is universal. Her weaving echoes in the Andean textiles dyed with earth and sky, in Navajo rugs that tell stories of balance, in African kente cloths that speak of identity and honour. Leadership, too, must be cross-cultural — woven with humility, curiosity, and reverence.

As we came out of the first COVID lockdown, I received a heart stitched by a beautiful grandmother living in Chennai, India. It had found its way to me with a necklace I had ordered whilst in India, the day after visiting the Gurdwara. I had found a wonderful, creative artist named Bharati who made traditional Indian ritual jewellery. Her studio was based in Chennai. I had chosen this necklace as a reminder of the holy moments of joy I had shared with my father. Two Corian spheres, etched with tiny, coloured sapphires. Each stone represents a beautiful memory of our time together. One sphere sits slightly higher than the other, lovingly watching over the one below. When I wear it, I think of my father and of us, caringly fused together forever.

Travelling by postal van, train, boat and air, the beautiful heart made by the grandmother from Chennai had carried its love gently across the world alongside my necklace. It had been made by Bharati's mother. Bharati and I had been liaising over WhatsApp. Just as the necklace was ready to post, COVID hit like a dark eclipse, and we were launched and plunged into lockdown. At the time, air postal services were stopped, making it impossible to send it to the UK from India. We messaged each other over weeks, keeping each other updated and sharing stories, including my story of Silk Elephant. Six months later, the necklace arrived. It had been given to Bharati's friend, who had travelled to Singapore from India, and was then posted on to me in the UK as restrictions lifted. This story is about women coming together in community, helping to bring my father's memory home. A weaving of compassionate threads. When I wear that necklace, not only do I remember the happy memories of my father, but also this wonderful reminder of its journey home.

When I opened the package, there was a vibrant handmade heart, made using local silk thread, often used in sarees. It carried within Bharati's mother's story, her land, her culture and her love. With it came a tiny note that simply said '**Pyaar se buna**' (woven with love). Against all odds, it had made its way from one mother's kitchen to another. This offer of love and kindness, in its simplest form, brings leadership to life as a tapestry—each thread holding its own history, but when intertwined, it creates a bond that stretches across borders and cultures. What began as a delivery of a necklace became a shared act of resilience, kindness, and trust.

In the second wave of COVID, I received a beautiful handwritten letter from an elderly care home in Ireland. It was a letter of thanks for having sent over 30 Christmas hearts to share love with their residents. In return, a 90-year-old resident had knitted a green heart. It wasn't perfect—wobbly and uneven—and it carried the words: *'You made me feel remembered'*.

That small, imperfect heart is also what leadership really looks like. It's what modern Bridget represents, reminding us that connection is never about perfection; it's about honest presence. Every stitch, every act, however humble, becomes part of the wider fabric. This is the essence of tapestry leadership—strong, not because the threads are flawless, but because they are bound together in love and belonging.

Weaving Love Into Leadership

Take five minutes to reflect on the values, relationships, and qualities that bring love and humanity into your leadership, and make them tangible through colour and creative.

PRACTICE Weaving Love Into Leadership

STEP 1: Gather Materials

- A handful of coloured ribbons, threads, or pencils (at least five different colours).
- A piece of paper or card.
- Optional: tape or glue if you want to create a physical weave.

STEP 2: Identify Your Threads

- On your paper, write down 3–5 'threads' you need to weave love into your leadership.

These could be:

- » **Values** (e.g., compassion, courage, integrity)
- » **People or relationships** (e.g., team, mentors, family)
- » **Practices or habits** (e.g., listening deeply, celebrating wins)

STEP 3: Assign Colours

- Choose a colour for each thread.
  For example:
  - » **Red** = Courage
  - » **Green** = Growth
  - » **Blue** = Calm

  If using ribbons or threads, lay them out in front of you. If using pencils, draw lines or shapes in those colours next to each word.

STEP 4: Weave or Draw

- **Option A (Physical Weave):**
  Tie or braid the ribbons together as you reflect on how these threads interconnect in your leadership.
- **Option B (Visual Weave):**
  Draw a simple weave pattern (like interlaced lines or a braid) and colour each strand according to your chosen threads.

STEP 5: Reflect

- *What does this weave tell you about your leadership?*
- *Where do you need to strengthen or add new threads?*
- *How can you keep these colours visible in your daily work?*

Before we move on to the people who hold you, take a quiet moment to listen inward.

Tending The Flame

Listening in the Quiet

Find a comfortable place to sit or stand

and soften your gaze.

Notice where stillness already exists in

your body—a pause between breaths,

a heartbeat, a sigh.

Rest your awareness there.

In that space of quiet,

the flame steadies itself.

You don't have to chase insight;

it finds you when you become

still enough to receive it.

Choosing Your Soul Threads – The People Who Hold You

When I started the charity, the first four women I reached out to helped build the inner framework of my tapestry. They were my soul threads.

- **Helen**, who always listened and supported, grounding me with compassion and calm truth, and, as a retired, yet young-at-heart fashion designer, brought with her the lived heritage of the beauty of textiles.
- **Karen**, a voice of reason and life experience—gentle, honest, sometimes brutally so. A corporate leader who, against all odds, went from being homeless as a young teenager to becoming one of the most successful HR board directors at the Bank of America.
- **Kay**, whose heart was open, generous, and giving. A gentle soul, always smiling and bringing with her years of heart-led leadership.
- **Katie**, a thread that shimmered with belief in others and carried us forward with warmth. A young woman with the strength to withstand the deepest of sorrows.

Katie was the young woman who, in silence and reverence, had placed the first handmade heart into my hand. It was a moment of pure humanity—no words, no instruction, just presence. A gesture that said: *I see you. I care. You are held.*

That heart was the seed of *Silk Elephant*. It was the moment that set everything in motion.

And now, as I write this, I smile at the synchronicity: Katie's married name is **Weaver**. There is a story in that. She didn't just give me a heart—she wove a moment. She carried Brigid with her, in name and in action. That first heart was handmade with love, and it became the thread that stitched together a movement.

I hold the connection with Katie dearly. At my father's funeral, attended by over 100 people whose lives he had touched, it was Katie's 100 handmade hearts that brought warmth, love, and precious memories into Dunham Crematorium. I remember that day not just with sadness, but with celebration. I wanted that day to bring my father's legacy to life—choosing to bring live music, poetry, Freddie Mercury, and the Beatles into his place of rest. Some thought I was mad, others were baffled by the thought, and yet on the day, it was glorious. A perfect moment in time. The energy of that day will reside in the chapel forevermore.

A live Beatles duo sang, *All You Need Is Love.* Every family member, friend, and former colleague who knew my father swayed to the music and sang. Not solemnly, but celebratory. With the strumming of guitars and the echo of heartfelt lyrics, we were bathed in love and remembrance. In that moment, radiant joy pierced the veil of grief, illuminating the darkest corners. I have never felt more present. The music didn't just fill the air—it filled us. It brought light into the dark and gathered every soul into a quiet, powerful unity.

Without Katie—without that silent moment of humanity, I would not have had the strength to bring that celebration together. It was her heart, that day on the Palatine ward, and the hearts that she crafted for the crematorium, that gave me the courage to celebrate rather than simply grieve. Her quiet offerings became a beacon and a reminder that grief, when held in community, can become a kind of grace.

This is what I want modern Bridget's to carry with them: the understanding that the threads of those people they choose are their connection to something beyond themselves. That in every connection we make, in every relationship we build—at work, at home, in community—we are weaving a tapestry of humanity. And in that weaving, we find strength, beauty and belonging.

Brigid's miracles were often quiet. So was Katie's.

Those first four women were the kind of allies Brigid herself might have gathered at her fire—strong women with clear eyes, fierce kindness, and hands ready to create and heal.

Without them, the seed of the idea would never have germinated. As I write, my tears are those of utter thankfulness. I am forever grateful. When I coach women, I like to invite them to think about who is within their core team, or as I call them, their soul threads or *Anam Cara.* These are the people who fully see them. These are the souls they can go to for shelter in a storm, or for celebration when they want to dance around the room. I have both sheltered, huddled together in my PJs with my *Anam Cara*, and danced like giddy kippers in the kitchen to the joyous words of 'Dancing Queen' by ABBA. They remain with us, both in times of darkness and in light.

Soul Friend

'You walked beside me
on the path of darkness,
held my trembling hand,
listened to the rain
as we searched the sky for stars.

We traced the soft moss
caressing the ancient oak
with fingertips,
and remembered together the ache of sorrow.

We welcomed silence.
In the stillness, you waited
inviting her softening voice
to heal me—
and in a miracle moment
the light came,
an outstretched ray of hope.
You ushered love back home'.

—Zoë

REFLECTION Threads of Belonging

Brigid, the tender weaver of hearth and hope, reminds us that belonging is sacred. It is not earned through achievement but felt through connection. In every thread we choose and every relationship we nurture, we stitch ourselves into a greater story.

- **Who are the soul threads in your life?** The ones whose presence feels like home, who see you clearly and hold your story with care? These are the companions who walk beside you, even when the path is uncertain, and dance like giddy kippers with you in celebration.

- **Who grounds you, lifts you, listens deeply?** These threads are sacred. They are the quiet mentors, the fierce friends, the gentle anchors who help you stay rooted and rise.
- **What would it mean to honour them as co-weavers?** To name their influence, invite their wisdom, and make space for their threads in your leadership journey? Brigid teaches us that the most beautiful tapestries are never woven alone.

Community Tapestries – Collective Weaving

A tapestry begins with intentionality. So many tapestries are woven within communities to represent their people and the stories of their community, much like the Irish Grown Wools Tapestry Project in County Kildare. This was brought together for the *Brigid 1500* celebrations—the 1500th anniversary of St. Brigid, bringing communities together in a stunning act of collaborative creation. Four handmade wool tapestries, created in living memory—known as *St. Brigid's Cloaks*—were lovingly crafted entirely from native Irish wool by over 950 participants, including 250 schoolchildren.

Local wool cooperatives supplied the raw material, while educational workshops led by Wool in School, in partnership with Creative Ireland and Kildare County Council, provided the space and tools for everyone to contribute. These cloaks were not only visually rich, with traditional Aran stitch borders hand-knit by experienced craftspeople and vibrant, textured panels made by children, farmers, and community members alike, but they were also woven from the fabric of relationship, heritage, and shared purpose.

This beautiful project models leadership as tapestry in action:

- It began with hundreds of individual contributions — each unique yet stitched together to form something greater than the sum.
- It blended voices across generations — the skilled with the novice; the young with the wise.
- It celebrated local materials and deep heritage while inviting everyone to take part in the story.

Leadership, like these cloaks, thrives when we choose threads that carry diverse stories, skills, and a sense of belonging. It is not about a single designer, but about the collective weaving — a practice of stewardship, co-creation, and honouring each contribution.

And so, in leadership, we must choose our threads, our people, to co-create and weave a tapestry that brings all those unique threads together for a richness of life.

The most accomplished weaver I know is a school friend, Kirsty James. She started weaving in primary school, asking the head teacher if she could start a lunchtime club for other students who were shy and, as she puts it 'quieter playground warriors'. She wanted to tend the hearth not just for herself, but for others. This selfless act of creating community has lived with her throughout her whole life. Kirsty has spent decades threading connection, compassion, and community into the fabric of her work. She is the founder and curator of TEDx Warrington — a long-held dream she brought to life in 2022, which brought to her home town this thriving and infamous global platform for showcasing 'ideas worth spreading'. Her leadership of a 30-strong team reflects her belief in legacy building through collective achievement. In 2020, Kirsty was honoured with the Prime Minister's Point of Light award for her extraordinary contribution to the community during COVID-19, coordinating support so that no one was left behind.

Kirsty's leadership is rooted in what she calls 'connecting with purpose'. She leads with fierce moral clarity, a pay-it-forward ethos, and a deep commitment to collaboration and care. As she said in her TEDx talk, 'Legacies are not just what we leave behind, but living and breathing micro-opportunities built from collective achievement'. I am always amazed by her relentless energy and her continual daily weaving. She is the embodiment of a modern Bridget, and I am humbled to call her a friend and to talk leadership with her. Her life tapestry is one of the richest I know, and you can see that from the endless vibrant LinkedIn posts and Facebook stories that gift us a wonderful peek into the window of her world. Kirsty reminds us that weaving change begins with choosing threads of purpose and people and weaving them with care.

But not all tapestries are woven with care. Sometimes, leadership fails to honour the threads it gathers. Sometimes, the loom is broken before the weaving begins.

I once consulted for a business where high-resolution prints of vision and values adorned every wall—bold statements of integrity, inclusion, and innovation. Yet behind closed doors, the culture told a different story.

In senior leadership meetings, women were spoken about in sexist, belittling ways. Pubs were discussed where non-white people were not welcome. The leadership was small-minded, exclusionary, and blind to its own hypocrisy.

This was a fractured business. Innovation was stifled, turnover was high, and within the industry, people spoke of them with a kind of weary knowing. The tapestry they claimed to weave was a facade—threads chosen for appearance, not substance. There was no true weaving of belonging, no celebration of difference, no stewardship of collective purpose.

Leadership in these moments requires more than a rebrand — it demands reckoning. It asks us to name what is broken, to listen deeply, and to begin again with humility and courage. It asks us to rethread the loom with care, and to invite every voice — not just the loudest — to shape the design.

In leadership, weaving a tapestry is more than a metaphor, it is a practice of connection, community, and care. Each thread we choose — each person we invite into our journey — adds texture, colour, and strength to the whole. Some leaders embody this weaving with extraordinary grace. One such leader is Emma Gaudern.

I was lucky enough to meet Emma Gaudern over 25 years ago, in my early career as a clinical negligence solicitor at Alexander Harris. We both started the same week and instantly became friends. Emma has infectious energy, and even back then, she was ambitious, sharp, and full of heart. We forged a bond after I performed the Heimlich manoeuvre when she choked on a pear — an unforgettable moment that somehow set the tone for a friendship built on trust, laughter, and shared purpose.

Today, Emma is the CEO and co-founder of EMG Solicitors, the largest independent Court of Protection firm in the UK. Her leadership is a masterclass in values-driven culture, led by soul. EMG isn't just a law firm — it's a community; a beautiful, rich, luminous tapestry. Under Emma's guidance, the firm has grown to manage over £400 million in client assets, supporting hundreds of vulnerable individuals with compassion, expertise, and integrity. But what sets EMG apart is not just its legal excellence — it's the culture Emma has cultivated. EMG has been recognised with B Corp certification, Investors in People Gold, and was listed in The Times and Sunday Times UK 100

Best Places to Work 2024, with 94% of colleagues saying they're proud to work there.

Emma's leadership is deeply human. She splits her time between running the firm and acting as deputy or trustee for clients, many of whom are navigating life with significant challenges. Her work is grounded in empowerment, helping people live life on their own terms. The firm's values—cooperation, courage, excellence, integrity, and kindness—aren't just words on a wall. They are lived daily, embedded in policies, performance, and relationships. EMG's culture supports flexible working, prioritises wellbeing, and actively gives back to the community. It's a place where people thrive, not just professionally, but personally. Emma is a modern Bridget—fierce, nurturing, visionary. Her tapestry is woven with threads of justice, care, and joy. And I am proud to have witnessed her journey from a young solicitor with a spark to a leader whose light now illuminates the lives of so many.

REFLECTION **Weaving with Heart**

1. **Who are the threads in your leadership tapestry?**

   How might you honour their threads in your own weaving?

2. **How do you cultivate belonging in your work?**

   Brigid tended the hearth—a place of warmth, welcome, and nourishment. Consider your own leadership spaces. Are they places where others feel safe to show up fully? What rituals, values, or practices help you create a culture of care?

3. **What legacy are you weaving?**

   Brigid's cloak was said to expand miraculously to cover all who needed shelter. What kind of legacy are you stitching into your leadership? Is it one of justice, kindness, and courage? What threads do you want to leave behind for others to carry forward?

Threads Across Oceans – A Tapestry of Shared Humanity

Sometimes you send a single thread across an ocean, and it weaves itself into something you could never have made alone.

That was the case when I reached out to Jacob Cramer, founder of *Love For Our Elders* in the U.S.A. Jacob had begun writing handwritten letters to isolated older adults during the COVID-19 pandemic. What surprised me most was his age—just 20 years old in 2020—and already leading a movement of compassion.

His charity began when he was only 13, inspired by the loss of his beloved grandfather and by the quiet loneliness he had witnessed among senior citizens. His grandmother, Doris, had a tradition of sending him heartfelt letters, and in her honour, he later established *National Letter to an Elder Day* on her birthday, February 26.

Within 48 hours of my LinkedIn message, Jacob and I were on a Zoom call, exchanging stories and weaving our visions together. Jacob had already gathered a small army of university students and volunteers, souls who were reaching thousands of older adults during lockdown. I was moved by his clarity and courage—and invited him into mine: an *International Kindness Exchange*.

I imagined love crossing the Atlantic. From the UK, we would send handmade hearts; from the U.S., Jacob's community would send handwritten letters. The only challenge? Ensuring our hearts were flat enough to slip into envelopes. Within an hour, we had a plan—and a promise.

Our eight Kindness Ambassadors rallied our network of creative volunteers to craft paper, cardboard, and foam hearts.

The ones that touched me most were made by two sisters, aged seven and nine, who used a heart-shaped cake cutter to stamp foam hearts full of joy.

The first package we sent held over 1,000 hearts, packed into a reused gift box from my son's 21st birthday lockdown. Weeks later, a matching package arrived—filled with more than 1,000 handwritten letters gathered through Jacob's charity. Opening it was like opening the most beautiful gift imaginable. My kitchen table became a sea of love. As I read through the letters, tears fell. Such tenderness. Such care.

The real gift came when a message arrived from the Culver City Council in California, thanking us and sharing that many hearts had been distributed across the city. This exchange was symbolic. It connected families, hospitals, and care homes across continents through shared humanity. Letters and hearts found their way into palliative care units, hospital wards, and family kitchens. In places where grief and loneliness had taken root, these threads carried warmth, comfort, and presence to elderly people.

Since then, Jacob's work has gained international recognition. In 2025, he was featured in the *Rad Human* segment on the *Kelly Clarkson Show*, and through his advocacy *National Letter to an Elder Day* is now officially recognised by Hallmark and the U.S. Postal Service. Just WOW! This is what happens when you find that spark, and the soul comes alive.

In that intentional weaving, we stitched a shared global message:

You are not forgotten. You are seen. You are held.

It remains one of the most soul-nourishing collaborations I have ever witnessed.

REFLECTION Threads of Global Compassion

- **Who are the threads you've woven from a distance?**

  Think of connections that have crossed borders, time zones, or cultures. What did they teach you about shared humanity?

- **How do you honour the invisible threads of kindness?**

  Consider gestures, messages, and acts of care that may seem small but carry deep meaning. How do you keep those threads alive in your leadership?

- **What legacy are you stitching into the global tapestry?**

  Brigid reminds us that every thread matters. What message do you want your work to send across oceans, generations, and hearts?

The Living Bridge—Leadership That Connects Through Storms

When I began my journey of writing poetry and listening deeply, my close friend, Molly, handed me a book. Molly has a particular way of knowing what you truly need. It's a gift of deep intuition. When she handed me *Belonging* by Toko-pa Turner, I had no idea how impactful that book would be on me. I savoured every page and walked a life journey with a most beautiful woman.

If you are trying to find the essence of who you are, struggling to find the light within, or simply want to take moments in stillness to witness an unfolding of connection and love, this book is a gentle guide.

In the opening pages, Toko-pa brings to life a sacred metaphor of connection through the living root bridges of the trees of

Meghalaya. It moved me so deeply that, one hour into the book, I scoured the internet for an original painting of the bridges. I wanted to convey the intertwining of nature's magic and the beauty of the human soul.

Two weeks later, a beautiful oil painting arrived, lovingly painted by an Indian artist who had visited Meghalaya many times. It now hangs opposite my bed. Most mornings, sunlight delicately illuminates the dark roots of the trees. It is a painted prayer, reminding me of the humanity and resourcefulness of community.

The living root bridges hold an ancient story. They have been in this region for hundreds of years, connecting people and wider communities during monsoon storms. When the rivers rise and are too high, and the current too strong to cross, the roots of the fig tree form a network of bridges. They are living tapestries, woven both for trade and sharing goods, and to prevent isolation and foster connection.

This is a true tale of bringing nature and community into harmony. The women and men in the Khasi and Jaintia hills tend the roots of the rubber fig tree (*Ficus elastica*), weaving them into bridges over rivers. These living structures take 15–25 years to form, but once grown, they can carry fifty people at once and endure for centuries.

These sacred living bridges were not built. They have grown. And they are still alive. They survive monsoons because they move with it.

So, too, in leadership: We don't construct. We cultivate. We don't stand apart. We weave into.

Brigid, who blessed rivers, healed wells, and connected the natural and spiritual realms, would have understood these bridges. She, too, was a bridge-builder across divides of gender, class, faith, and fear.

In leadership, you never truly know when a storm will hit. Tragic, unimaginable moments can arrive without warning—moments no strategic plan, risk register, or board meeting can prepare you for.

When the unthinkable happened in Southport in July 2024—the stabbing of three young girls and injuries to others during a children's workshop—the shock reverberated far beyond the town. For us, with a large office in Southport, it wasn't an abstract headline. It was heartbreak that touched our people directly. Colleagues had friends, neighbours, and even family connected to those affected.

In that moment, leadership was not about performance or planning. It was about humanity.

It was about how we held space for grief, fear, and anger. How we reminded our people that they were not alone. Our responsibility was to weave a net of care, to create living bridges—checking in, offering flexibility, providing support services, and simply being present. In a world fractured by violence, the true test of leadership is not how we command, but how we connect.

What astounded me was how our network of leaders stepped into a role they had never been trained for. Within hours, we had counselling services on site, peer support groups in place, and a senior leadership presence woven into a living network of care. We brought our physical selves to Southport with our executive heads and our caring hearts.. Our presence echoed through every act, every conversation, every broadcast during that difficult time.

None of this would have been possible without the foundations we had laid—the months and years of weaving rootedness into our leadership. We cultivated a culture where leaders are custodians of their people. This extends beyond 9 to

5, and into the wider landscape of life. Leadership, at its heart, is about being available, approachable, and present—especially when the storm hits.

I look back on that time with a sense of grace. If we could hold ourselves together in the face of such unimaginable tragedy, then whatever storms lie ahead, we will meet them with strength and soul.

I believe Brigid was with us through those dark days, ensuring that even in the deepest sorrow, the flame still held warmth so that soul-led leadership could still shine.

REFLECTION **The Sacred Weave of Leadership**

Storms will come. Some arrive quietly, while others roar in without warning. Leadership in these moments is about care. It concerns how we show up, hold space, and weave strength into the fabric of our communities. Let these questions guide your reflection:

- **When the storm hits, what anchors your leadership?**

  Is it your values, your people, your faith, or your lived experience? What roots do you return to when the winds rise?

- **How do you show up—not just as a professional, but as a human?**

  Do you bring presence, empathy, and vulnerability? Can you offer steadiness without needing to fix everything?

- **What networks of care have you woven in advance, and how do they hold during crisis?**

  Have you cultivated trust, connection, and psychological safety? Do your people know they are seen, supported, and held?

- **Who are the leaders around you who step forward with courage and compassion?**

  Who rises in the dark with a steady flame? Who listens deeply, acts gently, and leads with soul?

- **What bridges are you growing—slowly, patiently—to carry others through the storms?**

  Are you tending relationships that will endure? Are you weaving legacy through love, not just leadership?

Letting in Joy – The Thread that Brightens the Tapestry

I am deeply grateful for the laughter I share with my leadership peers. In those moments, we create space to exchange personal joys, express gratitude, acknowledge challenges, and simply show up as the beautifully human selves we are.

One of my favourite highlights is our annual fancy-dress dinner at the senior leadership retreat. It's an evening devoted to silliness and imagination — a chance to smile at each other's playful creativity. I often groan at first about choosing an outfit, but the moment I walk into the room dressed as Patsy from *Absolutely Fabulous*, I breathe. The weight of the day — strategy discussions and growth plans — melts away. We talk about life beyond work. This year, I spent a wonderful hour with one of our leading legal minds, laughing as she shared stories about her son's eclectic collection of pets — from lizards to hamsters to singing parrots.

These moments remind me that joy is a vital thread in the leadership tapestry. When we allow joy to enter, we soften the edges of hierarchy, strengthen connection, and create spaces where imagination and humanity can thrive. Joy is the golden thread that makes the weave shimmer.

REFLECTION

- Which thread represents joy in your leadership?
- How do you invite joy into your daily work?

INVOCATION

Weave a Tapestry

Every thread you choose is a prayer;

weave with love,

and the pattern will shine.

3

Step Into Your Beauty

Áilleacht*

* The Irish word for beauty is '**áilleacht**' (pronounced *aw-lyukht*).It's a rich, lyrical word that evokes not just physical beauty, but a deeper sense of grace, harmony, and soulfulness.

Step Into Your Beauty

Be real. Be human. Be you.

To lead is to be seen. This invitation asks us to embrace our wholeness—the radiant truth of who we are. It is a call to authenticity and individuality, to show up fully, and to honour the beauty that lives in our own divine story, our voice, and our presence.

Within Me

'Within me,
The universe resides,
Along with every life lived—
Both my own and those before me.
It is a temple of wisdom,
Love and compassion.
No other sanctuary is as sacred and beautiful
As my own self—
For how I love myself
is how I teach others
to love me,
And in that reflection,
the universe learns, too'.

—Zoë

Not a Return, But a Rising

Opening Reflection – Stepping Into My Beauty

There comes a quiet moment, often born of sorrow or age, when a woman no longer asks for permission to be herself. For me, that moment came in my fifties, following the death of my father, a difficult divorce, and a long road of inner healing. Woven through that journey was the unexpected joy of new love and the bold step into a new career path.

In December 2024, as I reached the fifth anniversary of my father's passing, I took a long weekend to sit with pen and paper and map the milestones of those five years. What emerged was a stark but nourishing reminder of the steps I had taken to become a woman who truly loved herself, deeply and beautifully.

In those five years, I divorced and moved into a home of my own. The first property to be solely mine. I remember holding the keys, trembling with both excitement and fear, about to cross a threshold into a life I had no idea how to navigate. During the time that followed, I found new love, remarried, and moved again, this time with a steadier heart.

In 2023, I closed the door on Zebra—my firstborn business, crafted with heart, passion, and twelve years of hard, grounded work. It wasn't a goodbye, but a parting thank you. A moment of reverence for all it had taught me.

I stepped into a C-Suite role at Fletchers, returning to the world of law—a place I never imagined re-entering, with its sharp edges and familiar corridors. But something in me had shifted. I was no longer seeking to build alone. I was ready to belong to something larger than myself.

It wasn't a return; it was a rising. A choice to lead from the soul. To carry the essence of Zebra with me, leaving aside brand, bringing a new way of being.

I had learned, through the rhythm of entrepreneurship, to walk into rooms with courage. I remember stepping into the glass lift of one of New York's largest investment houses. The city sprawled beneath me like a map of possibility. A voice whispered inside, *'How can I walk in here and talk business'?*

But I did. With my Manchester Bee notebook in hand, I spoke the truth. I didn't pretend my business was bigger than it was. I didn't claim credentials I hadn't earned. I simply shared my deep understanding of the legal sector and my willingness to adapt, learn, and serve.

That honesty won a five-year deal. It transformed my business. But more than that, it affirmed something sacred: When spoken with clarity and heart, truth opens doors no performance ever could.

By the end of 2024, I had completed a seven-year psychotherapy journey. I gathered the tools to live with complex PTSD as a landscape I had learned to navigate. The bathroom floor, once a place of despair, became a memory of survival. It became a quiet altar to resilience.

I looked back on those five years and whispered to myself; '*You didn't get it all right. But you were true. And I am proud'.*

Around this time, I rediscovered the poet, David Whyte. Years before, his work had warmed me but didn't ignite a fire. Then, in January 2025, I joined his Sunday series on renewal and was hooked. His words sang to the soul I had finally made space for.

His poetry became a companion. And in his voice, I began to hear my own.

That summer, in June, I joined one of his walking tours; an invitation to listen, not just learn. I immersed myself in nourishing words and silent, prayerful landscapes.

I went with no expectations, only a quiet intent: just to be. On the final morning, I sat by my bedroom window in the soft, forgiving light and I wrote in my journal:

> ***'I have spent this week with so many beautiful souls. But the most beautiful soul I have walked with is the one inside me. The one I have witnessed in silence. The one I have made space for. The one I have finally met with compassion'.***

That week, listening to David, I began to remember who I truly was. For much of my life, I wore many faces — masks I thought necessary to succeed or survive. On the first day, David introduced Fleur Adcock's beautiful poem *Weathering*. As he recited the lines, *'Now that I'm in love with a place that doesn't care how I look or if I'm happy, happy is how I look'*, the words buried themselves deep in my marrow. They became a powerful meditation on ageing, self-acceptance, and belonging to a place that asks only presence.

On the front of my journal, I wrote:

> ***'I am shedding the faces I have worn, so that I can wear joy'.***

The week wasn't about losing identity. It was about finally being ready to meet myself; to step into my beauty and happiness. Happiness doesn't ask for permission; it arrives when we do.

That week in the Lake District was more than a retreat; it was a full-circle moment. A breath of compassion after years that tested my resilience, leadership, and sense of self. It was a thank you to me for enduring, becoming, and finding the beauty within. What remained was no mask, but a light.

I call this chapter 'Step into Your Beauty' to speak not of image, but soul. It is about honouring and celebrating the emerging fullness of who we are: the courage to be seen, the grace to be still, the inspiration to lead with love, and the compassion to love ourselves.

Brigid's flame burns in every woman who dares to lead from her truth and own her becoming. Because when we do, we become beacons for those we lead in the boardroom, in the home, and in the world.

I write this invitation for every woman who has ever felt too much, too quiet, too bold, too soft. It is for the leaders who wear joy like a cloak, who walk into boardrooms in pink trainers, who whisper beauty into the hearts of others, and who hold their own hearts as a precious gift.

'When you let go of who you are,
you become who you might be.
When you let go of what you have,
you receive what you need.
When you let go of trying to be beautiful,
you become beautiful'.

– Rumi (paraphrased teaching)

INVITATION Rise as Brídget from Brigid's Flame

I invite you to rise with the light of Brigid's living flame, walking the path of life and leadership as bearers of beauty and grace.

- Carry her spirit with you, becoming a modern incarnation of all the wonder and diversity she embodied. As you walk in love, let her many guises live through you—modern Bridgets: women who transform, women who love, women who heal, women who walk the path of the soul.
- Let her rise in your voice when you speak truth in rooms that once silenced you.
- Let her rise in your stillness when you choose presence over performance.
- Let her rise in your joy, your softness, your fire.
- Step into your beauty. And rise.

The Faces We Wear

For years, I wore the faces I thought were required: lawyer, corporate, dutiful wife, good daughter, never 'too much'. I learned to read the room, mirror the tone, and soften my edges. I was successful, yes, but I was also edited.

And I wasn't alone.

As women in leadership, we are often taught to polish ourselves to perfection. I remember this vividly as a young lawyer. I was taught to speak well, but not too assertively. To be warm and inviting to clients and peers, but never weak. To be strong but not ruffle too many feathers. And to dress accordingly—not to express, but to conform.

So many of us spend our careers and our lives beyond the boardroom, shaping ourselves to fit a mould.

I often discuss this with my nineteen-year-old daughter, as she faces a world with little room for rawness. I wouldn't want to be a teenager in this era of relentless, polished social media, where adapting images is common, and wild, unfiltered beauty can be forgotten. With curated feeds and filtered faces, there is a quiet pressure to conform.

I invite you and your daughters to see beauty as the kind that lives in laughter lines, in the glow of presence, in the wildness of being real. When beauty presents unfiltered, it radiates.

I watch my daughter navigate this terrain with courage. And I remind her, often, that her realness is her radiance. That the world may try to edit her, but her soul was never meant to be cropped.

One evening at the cinema, this conversation deepened. The film explored a woman simply being herself — messy, unapologetic, awkward. My daughter lit up watching a woman with permission to be fully herself. It sparked joyful dialogue about authenticity: that awkward, brilliant character was a true modern Bridget.

When I sit with my daughter, I smile at her courage; the same raw, honest energy we saw in that film. If I had found that courage at her age, it may not have taken me until 52 to fully step into my own beauty.

When we put on a mask and wear the many faces we feel necessary to be accepted, understood, and embraced, we lose what makes us powerful — our realness. People are drawn to my daughter's genuineness; she lives without ego or pretence. She truly is a beautiful young woman. I try to help her see the magic in her beauty, and I see many women champion others' beauty but struggle to see their own.

I meet extraordinary women every day. Brilliant, capable, compassionate leaders who struggle to bring their whole selves to the table. They've been shaped by systems, mentors, and expectations that taught them to be less. Less emotional. Less colourful. Less intuitive. Less visible.

In my coaching practice, I often ask: *'What would it look like to bring your whole beautiful self to leadership'?* I've come to expect the pause that follows. It invites a moment of deep listening—a reaching inward toward something hidden. What they touch is tender. How they answer is brave.

Many become tearful. I give them space, and they give themselves permission to speak with courage. They speak of wanting to laugh more. To cry without shame. To wear colour. To speak up. To slow down. To lead with intuition. To stop apologising.

They speak of wanting to be real. And when they do, when they begin to step into their beauty, they come alive. The energy shifts. Their teams soften. Their cultures transform. Their impact deepens.

The courage to be human and real is contagious. When beauty is shared honestly, it soothes both the individual and the culture around them. We feel this truth in our bones. Research echoes it, too.

Leadership studies affirm what many women already know. Harvard professor Robin Ely and her colleagues describe how women often feel compelled to wear a 'mask of masculinity'. They perform traits like authority and confidence just to be seen as legitimate.

These masks come at a cost.

I've witnessed in coaching sessions how masks begin early. They are shaped in childhood, then reinforced in boardrooms. These masks form as protective layers. Tender at first, then hardened by expectation. With time, they become armour.

Sadly, armour, while it shields, also isolates.

These women — brilliant, capable, compassionate — lose themselves in the fog of overwhelm. Their teams struggle to breathe in open-hearted ways. Creativity dims. Connection frays. Joy becomes a distant echo. Yet, beneath the mask, the flame still flickers. It waits and wants to be seen. When a woman dares to remove the mask, even slightly, something shifts.

The room breathes.

The culture softens.

The flame of authenticity flickers into view.

This quiet revolution is not just felt; it's mirrored in research. Sally Helgesen and Marshall Goldsmith call it the *'perfection trap'* in their book, *How Women Rise*. I read it while travelling through the Outer Hebrides in June 2024. Paul and I had taken an extended three-week holiday. It was a time to pause, to breathe in the stillness of the land, to let the wind untangle what had been tightly held. I was four years into grieving my father's passing and one year into my new marriage. I could feel the healing power of courage beginning to take root. I was starting to love myself again.

I even noticed that my laugh had changed. It was freer somehow, giddier, and louder than it had been in years. A person's laugh can say so much about them.

The book spoke to me deeply, especially its reflections on perfection.

Perfection becomes another mask.

Women are taught not just to succeed, but to do so flawlessly — to edit themselves until only the polished parts remain. This pursuit silences creativity. It dilutes power. It exhausts the spirit. And beneath it all, the soul waits; unpolished, unedited, whole. Helgesen and Goldsmith speak of this exhaustion. Of the quiet grief that comes from being present but not known.

This is not a failure of the women.

It is a failure of the system.

Over this past year, I've coached a law firm Partner, Saima. Her vulnerability is magnetic. She leads with humility instead of ego. Her strength doesn't come from pretending; it comes from presence. In a world obsessed with image, her ability to be real is revolutionary.

Modern Bridgets like her are quietly yet powerfully reshaping the role model for leadership.

When you lead without pretending, you give others permission to do the same. You create space for trust. You build a culture where failure isn't fatal and growth is real.

I've watched Saima champion members of her team who were struggling;. Instead of trying to fix things for them, she believed in them. She stood up for them, guided them, and helped them see their own strengths. And in our coaching sessions, I've supported her in seeing her beauty through her own reflection.

The most powerful leaders are not those who shine alone, but those who help others see their light and remember their own.

REFLECTION **The Flame Beneath the Mask**

Brigid's fire is not about spectacle. It is about presence. About warmth. About the courage to be seen. When we hold the spirit of her flame within us, we walk forward with the light of grace.

- What are the masks you've worn to belong? The polished faces, the softened edges, the rehearsed lines? These masks may have protected you, but they were never meant to define you.
- Who are the people who see you without the mask—without your social facades? The ones who honour your awkwardness, your brilliance, your contradictions.

These are your truth-holders, 'your heart-circle', the people who recognise the real you and remind you that you are enough, even when you feel exposed.

- What would it mean to lead from that place?
- What if you let go of performing and step into presence?
- What if you became the kind of leader who not only shines but also warms; who not only speaks, but truly listens; who not only succeeds, but connects?

The Courage to Be You

It takes courage to remove the faces we wear and truly step into our beauty. For many years, I found it easier to say yes—to peers, to friends, to partners, to line managers. Easier to remain silent, even when something inside me longed to speak.

For over a decade, within a relationship, I learned to quieten my voice. After moments of discord, I chose silence as protection. Over time, this silence became like a mask, hiding my true self. When I finally set it aside, I learned to speak freely again and to laugh in a way that opened my heart. In doing so, I reclaimed the courage to be myself. The process of removing the mask began the moment I opened the door to my new home and entered the hallway—a symbolic crossing into a new phase of life. I remember the sun catching the edge of the bottom stair and feeling the presence of grace. It was a threshold moment; a crossing from one chapter to the next.

In Celtic tradition, thresholds are sacred. They represent quiet spaces of transition; between day and night, between seasons, and between what was and what is becoming. These thresholds are not just transitional moments, but invitations to growth and transformation.

Brigid herself is a threshold figure. She was born at dawn, between the old year and the new one. She stands between goddess and saint, between fire and water. She lives in the liminal—in the hush before the flame, in the breath before the word, in the stillness where transformation begins.

When I stepped into that home, I left behind the image I had created to preserve harmony and walked toward the truth of who I was. It was not always easy. Thresholds ask for courage. They ask for stillness and trust. They also offer transformation.

When we cross the threshold into authenticity, we begin to lead differently. We speak more clearly, listen more deeply, and create with more joy. We become not just leaders, but keepers of the flame, tending the light of truth in ourselves and in others.

When we choose to be authentic, our approach to leadership changes. We communicate more clearly, listen more attentively, and find more joy in what we create. We move beyond simply leading and start to nurture honesty in ourselves and those around us.

I invite you to find your own threshold—step forward, embrace your authentic self, and trust the transformation that awaits.

Butterflies of Light

'I stood and faced the lion,
and roared the unspoken fear —
My words released,
turning butterflies into light,
taming the lion, as they fluttered
delicately with each breath
the light within me grew strong,
my heart opened
and my soul danced.
Now I sing with the lion
and the lion sings with me'.

—Zoë

If something important is left unsaid because we struggle to find our voice, everything that follows is less truthfully spoken.

I remember a leadership meeting years ago when a colleague proposed a strategy that felt misaligned with our values. I felt it; the tightening in my chest, the quiet ache of silent knowing. Regretfully, I said nothing. I softened my edges, smiled, and stayed silent. That silence echoed. It shaped the meeting's tone and the decisions that followed. It shaped how I showed up: cautious, half-present.

Later, I realised my silence had not protected harmony. It had diluted truth.

Now, I speak when I need to. Even if my voice trembles. Even when the lion roars. Because when truth is spoken with love, it doesn't divide; it liberates. There is such joy in the song of our truth.

REFLECTION

- When did you last sing?
- What have you left unspoken out of fear of being you?

The Joy of Being You

Earlier this year, I published a post on LinkedIn titled *The Joy of Pink*, featuring a photograph of me, radiant with delight, wearing my favourite pink Adidas trainers to a boardroom meeting. What struck me was the fiery surge of engagement, especially from women. My joy clearly ignited something deep within them.

I shared that I wore my pink Adidas not just for comfort

(though they delivered on that, too), but as a conscious, small act of joy. I suppose you could say they were a quiet rebellion, a gentle defiance of the leadership norms I grew up with in the '90s. Back then, women in leadership often wore grey suits and shoulder pads, toning down their femininity to be 'taken seriously'. As a young lawyer, I found it stifling.

How far we've come

Those pink trainers were more than footwear. They were liberation. A symbol of freedom. Authenticity. Beauty. There is a wild joy in reaching the moment when your clothing sings your happiness. Where you no longer dress to impress, but to express. This is what the pink trainers meant to me. They were more than shoes. They were a declaration. A whisper of joy. A flash of truth. A reminder that beauty is not something we apply; it is something we unleash.

Now I choose colour. I choose comfort. I choose to lead with energy, joy, and presence. I don't want to blend in. I want to invite others in. When we're real, we make it safe for others to be real too.

Often, it's the small things that keep us grounded; the flashes of colour in a sea of grey, the pink trainers in the boardroom, the joy we carry with us, on purpose.

Walking the long road to my own becoming, I feel a steady pulse inside—a woman who knows and trusts herself. I invite you to listen for that heartbeat, too.

Every day, I witness courage in women. In the quiet moments of coaching, when a woman finally says, *'I'm tired of pretending'.* The electric silence in the boardroom, when someone dares to ask the question everyone fears. The glowing pride when a daughter chooses to be herself, even when the world tells her to be someone else.

This courage is contagious. It creates space. It builds trust. It changes culture.

There comes a moment in every woman's leadership journey when the masks begin to feel heavy. When the roles we've played, the ones we thought we had to wear to be accepted, respected, or safe, start to crack.

I've come to understand that authenticity is a daily practice. A quiet, courageous choice to let go of who we think we're supposed to be and embrace who we truly are.

It's not always easy. Sometimes it means speaking up when silence feels safer. Sometimes it means showing emotion in rooms that reward detachment. Sometimes it means choosing joy, colour, or softness in spaces that expect polish and control.

But when we choose authenticity, we become more than leaders—we become mirrors. We show others that it's safe to be real. That truth is welcome here. That beauty lives in the unedited self. Courage and authenticity walk hand in hand. We know when we encounter the real thing and we also know when we don't.

I've been in leadership meetings where someone pretended to have all the answers, and you can feel the barrier it creates. I've been to networking events where women arrived with a carefully polished story that didn't exist and the absence of truth was unmistakable. In those moments, the opportunity for connection is lost.

Pretense erodes trust. Courage—even imperfect, vulnerable courage—builds it.

Brené Brown reminds us that the original definition of courage comes from the Latin word *cor*, meaning heart. To lead with courage is to tell the story of who you are with your whole heart.

Courage is not always soft. Sometimes, it arrives as *rage*.

For women, rage can be a sacred signal; a fierce knowing that something in society is deeply wrong. It is not the opposite of love, but its protector. Rage, when rooted in truth and compassion, becomes a force of transformation.

I saw this courage — this transformative rage — in the women who supported my charity. Our eight Kindness Ambassadors weren't polished executives or boardroom-level CEOs. They were real women — honest, creative, and brave. Their courage wasn't loud or polished; sometimes, it carried the quiet weight of exhaustion, and at other times, the fierce energy of rage.

Together, they built a network of more than 700 volunteers and delivered over 110,000 hearts, gifts, and care packages across the world. On our Zoom calls, they spoke openly about feeling overwhelmed, uncertain, and saddened by COVID's impact on health, well-being, and community. They had the courage to lean into difficult conversations with one another and their volunteers about how to package care safely, prevent infection, and avoid rejection from hospitals and care homes.

It may sound simple, but in a volunteer-led environment, honesty and vulnerability take courage.

COVID created a highly charged atmosphere — stressful, emotive, fertile ground for ego. But these women chose another way. They let go of who they thought they should be, and in doing so, they created something sacred: community.

Their honesty built trust. It nurtured support, respect, and the determination to dig deep. Courage was at the heart of the charity's success. It was a quiet and graceful courage — the kind that shows up. The kind that says, *'I don't have all the answers, but I'm here. I care. Let's do this together'.*

This is the courage of women who rage with love. Who lead with truth. Who transform the world by becoming the beautiful souls they were always meant to be.

REFLECTION The Courage to Be You

- What parts of yourself have you hidden to belong?
- What truths have you silenced to stay safe?
- Who are the people who invite you to be fully yourself—no mask, no performance, just presence? These are your soul mirrors. Your truth companions.

'You do not have to be good.
You only have to let the soft animal
of your body love what it loves'.

—Mary Oliver (from* 'Wild Geese'*)

The Beauty of Your Values

Living your values means acknowledging the divinity of your own inner beauty.

When I began my executive coach training at Henley Business School, we were asked to complete an online values-based questionnaire. When my report pinged into my inbox, I was eager to see what it revealed. My initial reaction was surprise: it listed **love** and **kindness** as my top two values.

I felt deflated. I had expected something more dynamic, perhaps ambition, leadership, or resilience. But then I paused. I sat back and listened to what it was really saying. Behind the hard-won professional face I had worn for so long, this was the truth of who I was. This was the woman I had hidden.

Now, I feel proud. Love and kindness were central to my charity, symbolised by hearts and embodied in my connection with Katie. That was the real me.

I believe my leadership now embodies both love and kindness. Getting to that place has fed my soul and helped me step into my beauty.

When we don't live and lead by our values, our soul suffers. We feel distant from courage, from creativity, and from joy.

I invite you to reflect on the quiet truths that guide your decisions, shape your relationships, and define your leadership. When we know our values, not just intellectually, but from a deep place of knowing, we begin to live with integrity. We stop performing and start aligning. Approval becomes irrelevant. What matters most becomes clear.

Your values are your compass. They connect your inner world to your outer actions. When you lead from them with clarity, courage, and compassion, your beauty shines.

Take a moment to ask yourself:

- What are the values that feel most alive in me?
- Where in my life am I honouring them and where am I betraying them?
- What would it mean to lead in a way that reflects my deepest truths?

Brigid's flame is more than a symbol of authenticity; it is a symbol of values lived. Of truth spoken. Of love embodied. When we lead from our values, we become the flame.

Beauty Beyond Biography

So often, when we think about identity, we trace the lines of our biography: where we were born, what roles we've played, the successes and the failures that have shaped us. But identity is not the same as biography.

There is a place within you that your biography can't touch. A place untouched by criticism, rejection, or failure. A place of sureness, seamlessness, and quiet confidence. This is the heart of your identity. It is your inner flame, steady and unbroken, no matter what storms have passed through your life.

To step into your truth is to step into a place of divine inner beauty.

Every woman has luminous inner beauty guiding her life. It is the seat of our values, passion, and purpose, shaping how we live and lead from the soul. Belonging differs from fitting in. Belonging means embracing our wholeness, rather than exchanging it for acceptance.

Beauty is not glamour. It is not the curated images of perfection that surround us on cinema screens and social media posts. True beauty is what radiates when we learn the art of *in-withness*—when we live from within ourselves rather than chasing validation outside of ourselves. Beauty is the enriched memory of life: the tenderness we have known, the resilience we have carried, the compassion we have chosen.

When we mistake beauty for outwardness, we are left endlessly chasing, polishing, and editing. But when we understand beauty as something we draw from within, it becomes a wellspring. A place to return to. A source of leadership that is real, not performed.

This is what it means to step into your beauty: to know that your identity is not what has happened to you, but what lives in you. Lead from your true self, not just your life story.

In-Withness

'In-withness is the art of loving
from the inside out.
It is the silent knowing
that rises from your soul,
the breath that speaks
before the words,
the presence that doesn't perform
but simply is.
It is not about being seen—
it is about being met.
Not about being polished—
but being whole'.

—Zoë

The Flowering of Individuality – A Leadership Reflection

To be an individual is to stand apart; not in isolation, but in integrity. It is to resist systems that call us to conform. It means honouring the quiet voice within that longs to be true. This is not just a personal journey. It is the foundation of authentic leadership.

Leadership is often mistaken for fitting into a mould. It speaks the language of strategy and wears the uniform of success. Too often, it is performing the role others expect. Real leadership, though, begins when we choose to belong to ourselves. It is born in the tension between wanting to be accepted and longing to be free.

There is a contradiction we carry: the yearning to belong, and the longing to be ourselves. Real belonging is not found in the crowd or behind the mask. It is found in the soul. It is the moment we choose to belong to ourselves. We learn to fit into the world we've chosen. Over time, this becomes the norm. Sadly, the norm is not always nourishing. The soul, though, even when quiet, remembers. Often, it takes a rupture—a crisis, a loss, a moment when the ground beneath us gives way—to bring that remembrance. For me, it was the death of my father and a painful divorce, arriving like twin storms. In their wake, a clearing emerged. I could finally see my individuality as a gift. To honour it meant stepping into vulnerability and new horizons. When I looked closely—deep into the flower that was ready to bloom—I found creativity waiting. The raw kind. The kind that grows from the cracks and carries the beauty of the flaw.

For me, that creativity came as poetry. It was the courage to start anew, to write the truth in this book, to live forward and inward. The flowering of individuality is not all light; it asks us to lean into the shadows, to explore the soil from which beauty grows, and to meet the parts of ourselves we've hidden, softened, or silenced.

A living example of this is a close friend, Tamsin. She had once lived in a marriage that bruised more than her skin. Her desire to be financially independent, to become a lawyer, to pursue her ambition, was not accepted by her husband. The violence she endured culminated in a beating so severe it landed her in hospital—a moment that cracked open the possibility of escape. That weekend, I offered her refuge. She arrived carrying nothing but a small bag and a thousand unspoken fears.

Her family was split down the middle. Some urged her to stay, to forgive, to endure. Others stood ready to help her leave, though their support came with its own complexities. In the stillness of that weekend, she found the courage to choose herself. She asked for a divorce, knowing it would mean severing ties with half of her family. It was a painful liberation.

Tamsin longed to be free. And she chose freedom.

Years have passed. She is now a successful lawyer, a brilliant speaker, and remarried to someone who sees her light and never tries to dim it. I've watched her bloom—her laughter fuller, her presence stronger. She walks with grace and resilience, a woman who turned survival into sovereignty.

Tamsin's story is more than personal healing. It is one of leadership—leading herself out of harm, into truth, and becoming a beacon for others.

This is the flowering of individuality. And this is the kind of leadership our world needs.

I invite you to reflect: *What part of yourself is ready to bloom? Will you take the first step to honour it?*

PRACTICE for Stepping Into Your Beauty

- **Daily Reflection**: Ask yourself, *'What part of me did I hide today'?* and *'What part of me did I honour'?*
- **Joy Rituals**: Wear something that makes you smile. Speak a truth. Share a story. Dance.
- **Deep Listening**: Practice listening to yourself. What does your body say? Your breath? Your silence?
- **Beauty Journaling**: Write about moments when you felt most alive, most seen, most beautiful—not in appearance, but in essence.
- **Leadership Invitations**: Ask your team, *'What helps you feel safe to be yourself here'?* and *'What beauty do you bring to this work'?*

Always remember in your heart these three things . . .

'Where you come from

Who you are

What shall become of you'. *

---

* Paraphrased from the Kildare Poems c,14th century.

Letting in Joy – Wildness as Sovereignty

Five years ago, I stopped the never-ending ritual of straightening my hair! The daily effort to tame my curls into submission had been a way to smooth away my wildness. It was a way to appear more polished, more pleasing and safer. Sleek, straight hair — not too short, not too long — was a way of belonging.

When I walked into my new home in 2021, I crossed a threshold, and with it came a quiet rebellion. I rediscovered curly me again. I let my curls breathe. I let myself welcome the wild spiral of not just my hair, but the unruly, unapologetic, and a little bit crazy me! I found joy.

Now, when I look in the mirror at my mad curls, I feel alive, untamed, and whole.

I also found joy in finding my full and honest voice. I'm known for letting the occasional swear word land in a way that gives the moment weight. My friend, Molly, would call these my 'it's a shitter' moments! Those moments when only the joy of that word is appropriate. When it says everything that everyone else feels yet dares not say.

In my younger years, I would have worked hard to hide these 'it's a shitter' moments. But I don't want to hide them. I grew up with swearing — in the right places, never gratuitous. It's part of my heritage, part of my father's voice echoing through my life. I no longer feel shame or disgust about bringing that heritage into my world. Of course, there are times when it's not appropriate, and I'm wise enough now to know the difference.

These small acts — wild curls, honest words — are thresholds into joy. They are more than just triviality. They are sovereignty. Golden reminders that beauty is something we unleash. I call these my 'flinging off the bra' reminders! Letting the whole of who we are be naked and beautiful.

Joy is sometimes the way we wear our hair, the colours we choose, the words we speak without apology. These are acts of liberation. They are thresholds into authenticity. For me, every curl and every swear word became a manifesto: a declaration that I would no longer shrink to fit. Now I lead, love, and live from the truth of who I am.

When we become the wilder version of ourselves, we speak with more courage, lead with more creativity, and we invite others to do the same.

PRACTICE **Letting In the Wild**

- What part of you have you been straightening or silencing?
- What joy would you find in letting in the wild parts of you?
- What small acts are your sovereignty?

INVOCATION

Step Into Your Beauty

Forge your truth

like molten metal—

shaped by fire,

tempered by grace.

4

Lean Into Your Shadows

Scáileanna *

* The Irish shadows is '**scáileanna**' (pronounced *skaw-lanna*). It's the plural form of '**scáil**', which means *shadow*. Like many Irish words, it carries poetic resonance — often used in literature and myth to evoke mystery, depth, or the unseen.

Lean Into the Shadows

Befriend the darkness within.

Brigid tended both fire and well—light and depth. This invitation welcomes the shadow, not as something to fear, but as a source of wisdom. It invites curiosity, courage and the grace to explore what lies beneath the surface at the very heart of who we are. In the places of doubt and insecurity, we find the truth.

Beauty is in All That is Hidden

'Every flower blooms from the dark,
from the soil, from the silence, from the unseen.
Truth begins not from the light we show
but in the roots, we've buried,
the stories we've silenced,
the parts we've hidden to belong.
Beauty lives there,
not in the polished petals,
but in the flaw, in the fracture,
in the place where light breaks through.
To lean into the shadow
is not to be in fear of them,
but to walk beside them, to listen,
to let them speak gently.
When we befriend our shadow,
We reveal the light of compassion
And welcome our own belonging'.

—Zoë

Duality – The Lived-in Human Experience

Opening Reflection – The Shadow that Shaped Me

• • • • •

Looking back, I see that my life has always held both shadow and light. Sadness and joy. Life and death. Hope and resignation. Love and indifference. These dualities have coexisted since early childhood, shaping how I see the world and how I lead within it.

My earliest memory of shadow came after my mother, Diana, attempted suicide. Life had become too much, and in that moment, she saw no other way out. I don't recall the vivid imagery of the event, but I remember the overwhelming sadness that followed. I read it in the faces and energy of those around me: my elder brother, my father, my grandmother. The air was heavy with sorrow. Once you've experienced that depth of sadness, it never truly leaves you.

Brigid's spirit gently arrived in my life for the first time.

From that sorrow, something beautiful began to emerge within me. A quiet compassion. A longing to love. A tender instinct to hold moments of deep sadness with grace and to be present with them. I have soft, enduring memories of sitting on my mother's knee, holding her close, feeling her pain and wanting to soothe it. That instinct, to hold, to care, to understand, to heal, began to take shape in the quiet corners of my being.

It didn't bloom in the light. It appeared from the shadows, from the ache, the silence, the softness of sorrow. It became part of my foundation.

I invite you to think about any childhood or early adulthood shadows that have helped shape your foundation.

Heart First

It wasn't until my mid-40s that I fully understood the impact of that moment and its aftermath. When someone close to me experienced severe depression, I didn't feel the shame that others seemed to carry. I felt only love. A deep, unwavering compassion. I believe this is why love and kindness are the essence of my being, not just personally, but in how I lead. To lead from the heart first, as love.

Leadership is often spoken about in terms of strength, clarity, and vision. My experience is that true leadership also needs tenderness. It asks us to hold space for vulnerability so that courage can flourish. It asks us to honour the duality within ourselves and others. To lead from presence, with compassion.

The heart of human experience is not found in choosing light above shadow, but in learning to hold both tenderly and truthfully. To lead with love, even when the path winds through darkness. To offer kindness, even when the world feels unkind. And to remember: the most powerful leaders are often those who have walked beside the shadows, leaned gently into their contours, and chosen to bloom anyway.

When the shadow of deep sorrow entered my life once more, Katie placed her handmade heart silently into my hand. In that instant, something beautiful emerged: a long-buried memory of the silent love I once held for my mother. The heart carried the light of love and beauty. And Brigid's spirit walked beside me again, just as she had in my childhood. Her presence was quiet, but unmistakable: a thread of grace woven through pain, a whisper of love in the shadow's fold.

REFLECTION Holding Both

- What would it mean to honour the whole of your story, both the light that others see and life's shadows that shape you?
- How would you lead from what the shadows taught you?
- How would you lead from the heart if you trusted that the sorrow and the joy live side by side and that both have made you who you are?

The Shadow Within

Shadow isn't just found in the events that happen to us; it also lives quietly *within* us. It dwells in the tender tension between who we are and who we long to become. This inner conflict can make us turn away from our own depths, afraid of what we might uncover. Yet it is precisely in those hidden corners, the places we try hardest to avoid, that wisdom waits.

The shadow lurks quietly, deceives cleverly, hides deeply, and tricks us into believing stories about who we are and what we can or cannot do. It drives us towards addiction, whispers harsh judgments, and fuels the inner critic. It leads us into hypocrisy, causing us to violate our own boundaries and our integrity. The gentle truth is that we are *all* of it. The light *and* the shadow. The grace *and* the fire.

How could we know courage if we had never met fear?

How could we honour love if we had never felt its absence?

To live fully, we must uncover and embrace all of who we are. Not just the polished parts that we want others to see, but the raw, the real, the hidden. Only then can we lead with wholeness.

We've been conditioned to fear the shadows — both in life and in ourselves. By fearing them, we allow them to grow unchecked. Like ivy laced with poison, they begin to twist around the beauty within, choking our creativity, our joy, our dreams. And yet every aspect of who we are bears gifts of wisdom.

Befriending all my shadows, without and within, has been the most transformational part of stepping into my beauty; loving the whole, real me. It has been a tender journey, one that has led me to my most authentic self: a place where I feel at home, where I recognise both my strengths and my wounds, and where I can honour the beauty that lives within.

'To honour all of who I am
is to see my full beauty.
To befriend my own shadows
with compassion is to become whole'.

— Zoë

How beautiful would you be if you held your shadows with love?

Brigid and the Archetype of Integration

When I read *In Brigid's Footsteps* by Linda McFadden, I felt her words give language to what I had long felt: that Brigid is not only a saint or goddess, but a living archetype; a symbol of the Divine Feminine who walks with us through the liminal spaces of transformation. She tends both flame and well: the fire of courage and creativity, and the depth of healing and truth.

Brigid's archetype doesn't ask us to fix the shadow—she invites us to befriend it. She reminds us that wholeness is found in integration. In the weaving together of light and shadow, wound and wisdom.

My charity, Silk Elephant, helped me become curious about the entirety of me, and to begin weaving. Working alongside so many women, each carrying their own challenges and wounds, yet radiating strength. Their stories gave me the courage to ask the deeper questions. In their resilience, I found the bravery to let go of who I thought I was. And in that letting go, I began to see more clearly: to ask whether my marriage was truly enabling me to be everything I needed to be and what parts of me needed to heal before finding love again.

Looking back, I see now that the charity's journey didn't just support others, it quietly affirmed my own. It reminded me that the path I've walked, through grief, guilt, and self-doubt, was a sacred unfolding. A journey of integration. A journey Brigid herself might walk beside.

When we turn toward the shadow with quiet courage and loving compassion, there is a gentle shift. We begin to befriend the parts of ourselves we've hidden or silenced, and in doing so, we reclaim them. We begin to see that our strength lies not in chasing perfection but in wholeness. In understanding and welcoming all parts of ourselves with love. From this place of wisdom and self-compassion, genuine leadership is born — the kind that serves others and helps them to find their strength in wholeness, too.

Sit quietly and notice where light and shadow meet within you. Which parts of yourself have been hidden, and what might happen if you invited them into awareness without judgment? Let Brigid guide you to see that wholeness is not perfection, but the tender weaving together of every thread of your story.

Shadow Work and Leadership

To lead is to walk with both light and shadow. To hold space for complexity. To receive the silent gifts, like Katie's heart, and allow them to guide us back to love.

If we are to lead with authenticity, we must learn to walk with our shadows as teachers. The parts of ourselves we've hidden, feared, or judged often hold the very wisdom we need to lead with courage and compassion.

Shadow work is not a detour from leadership. It is the path.

When we avoid our inner conflicts — the grief, the shame, the fear — we risk projecting them onto others. We lead from defence, and in doing so, we miss depth. But when we turn inward, when we meet the shadow with curiosity rather than fear, we begin to lead from wholeness.

Consider a moment in your leadership when fear, doubt, or discomfort shaped your choices. How might that moment have shifted if you approached it with curiosity rather than judgment?

One leader I worked with avoided giving honest feedback,

worried it would make her appear weak. When she explored the shadow behind that fear, she discovered a deep desire to protect her team from discomfort. Leaning into that shadow allowed her to communicate with presence and empathy, transforming not only her relationships but also her team's trust and resilience. What wisdom might your shadow hold for your next step as a leader?

What Is a Shadow?

A shadow is not always dramatic. It's often quiet. Subtle. It lives in the places we avoid, the stories we don't tell, the emotions we suppress to stay safe or accepted.

It might be:

- The moment you said yes when your soul whispered no.
- The silence you held in a meeting because you feared being seen as 'too much'.
- The inner critic that tells you you're not ready, not qualified, not enough.
- The guilt you carry for choosing yourself.
- The resentment that simmers when your boundaries are crossed.
- The perfectionism that masks your vulnerability.
- The fear of being ordinary, or of being extraordinary.

Sometimes, the shadow is a belief:

- 'I must always be strong'.
- 'If I slow down, I'll fall behind'.
- 'I don't deserve joy until I've earned it'.

Sometimes, it's a memory:

- A moment of rejection.
- A time you felt unseen.
- A choice you regret but haven't forgiven.

Shadow work invites us to meet these parts to listen. To ask:

- *What are you here to teach me?*
- *What part of me needs love right now?*
- *What truth have I silenced that's ready to be spoken?*

Meeting the Shadow Through Reflection

I've already introduced you to the moment I met my own Gollum, reflected in another woman, and of what I feared I might become. That day in the law firm, when a senior colleague spoke with pride about dictating emails from her hospital bed during childbirth, something in me recoiled. Her story was framed as dedication, but I felt only sadness. It was a moment that revealed the shadow of a system that asks women to trade soul for status, and the shadow within me that feared I might do the same.

That experience stayed with me because she was a mirror. She showed me the part of myself that was still seeking approval, still afraid of being seen as less-than, still unsure whether choosing presence over ambition would cost me belonging. This is the essence of shadow work in leadership. It's not about judging others. It's about recognising the parts of ourselves we've disowned and reclaiming them with compassion. When we do this, we begin to lead differently. We begin to lead from truth.

'The shadow is the sacred twin of your light;
it softens the brilliance, so others may approach,
and you may come home to yourself'.

– Molly Harvey, The Mystic in Nature

Think of a moment when you have judged others' behaviours or choices. If you look in the mirror, what does it reveal about your shadow? How can you see the beauty in that?

'To hold a mirror up to yourself
with compassion is to reveal
the wisdom in your shadow,
to hide no more from
the full beauty of who you are'.

—Zoë

When We Hide from the Shadow

As we go through life, we are often taught to avoid the darker parts of ourselves. We learn to fear these parts, worrying they might be too painful or make us feel unworthy. We may believe that letting in anger will take away our ability to love, or that being imperfect means we can't be good parents, leaders, or role models. It can feel like no matter what we do, we can't escape this shadow.

Unless we befriend our shadow and get curious about it, it will quietly grow. It will take hold. And over time, it will begin to dim our light and obscure the beauty within us. When we deny parts of ourselves, the shadow doesn't disappear; it deepens.

I've learned through experience that this work requires gentleness. It asks us to look inward with compassion, not judgment. That's why I chose the phrase *lean into the shadows* — not to fight them, not to conquer them, but to meet them. To acknowledge that they are part of us. That they never fully go away.

When we lean in, we step out of the binary of good versus evil, light versus dark. We stop trying to beat the shadow and instead begin to understand it. And in that understanding, we reclaim our wholeness.

For many years, I lived with the quiet ache of guilt and shame. I stayed in a marriage where our arguments hurt not just us, but also affected the atmosphere our children lived in. I felt guilty about what they witnessed and ashamed that I couldn't fix it. I worried that I had failed them. That I had failed myself.

There were moments I questioned everything — my choices, my strength, my worth. I feared that staying had caused harm, and that leaving would too. The shadow of guilt whispered that I wasn't a good mother. The shadow of shame told me I wasn't a good woman.

But over time, I began to lean in. I began to be gentle with myself. To stop the self-blame and replace it with curiosity. I asked myself: *What was I trying to protect? What did I believe I deserved? What did I fear most?* And slowly, I began to see that guilt and shame were signposts. They pointed to the places within me that needed healing, compassion, and truth.

Working through that experience didn't erase the shadow.

It softened it. It gave me language. It gave me empathy. It was not a linear process. It was layered, tender, and at times, deeply uncomfortable. But it was also transformative. And now, when guilt or shame rises again, as it sometimes does, I no longer run. I lean in. I listen. I remind myself that leadership begins with self-forgiveness. That beauty includes the broken places. That Brigid walks with us, both in the light and in the fire of transformation.

Through both experience and study, we learn that the shadow is not something to be feared or exiled. One of the most beautiful gifts I received two years ago was Deepak Chopra's *The Shadow Effect.* It helped me make sense of the shadows I have faced and still live within me. His words, 'You cannot fight darkness with darkness. You have to turn on the light,' are still written on a note in my purse. It invites remembrance that the light is awareness. Compassion. Curiosity.

The shadow is not our enemy. It holds our unmet needs, unspoken truths, and wounded stories. When we choose to listen rather than try to fix, we start to reclaim the power we once lost.

Chopra speaks of the shadow as a spiritual teacher. It shows us where we are split, where we are hiding, and where we are ready to grow. For me, guilt and shame were not signs of failure; they were signs of depth. They revealed how much I cared. How much I longed to protect. And how much I needed to forgive myself.

Now, when those feelings rise again — as they sometimes do — I no longer resist them. I lean in. I ask: *What is this here to teach me? What part of me needs love right now?* And in doing so, I honour the shadow as a doorway to a place within me where I can walk in both light and dark. I can wander into the shy parts of myself with love and compassion.

★ ✶ ★

'The self is not a battlefield, but a wood
to be wandered, where light dapples dark,
and both are needed to truly see'.

—Graham Wiltshire, The Mystic in Nature

'Brigid, flame of quiet grace,
hold me in the places I've hidden.
Where guilt has lingered, and shame has grown,
let your light be soft —
a warmth that welcomes me home.
Teach me to live with tenderness,
to embrace myself with love and
to see the beauty in the broken,
and the wisdom in the wound.
To lead from love, even when I tremble'.

—Zoë

Brigid Guiding Questions

- What part of your story have you hidden in shadow, and what would it mean to hold it with compassion instead of shame?
- Where in your life have you mistaken guilt for failure, and how might you see it as a doorway to healing?
- What truth inside you wants to be spoken — not fixed or justified, but simply honoured?

The Throne Room and the Inner Room

I remember standing outside the throne room at Buckingham Palace, waiting to receive my MBE. My name had been called, my citation read aloud, and yet inside, I was asking myself: How did I get here? What did I really do?

The imposter's voice was loud.

I thought of all the years I'd worked quietly with charities, never seeing it as anything more than service. I thought of Silk Elephant, the charity I founded. I was comfortable acknowledging it was the seed of my idea, but felt the success of it was the sum of everyone else's efforts. I really didn't feel like I belonged in a palace. As I entered the throne room, I felt like a fraud.

And then it was Princess Anne.

She spoke of humility, kindness, and selflessness. She spoke of how much I had given in service whilst juggling a family and work. She thanked me for my compassion and love for others. Her words didn't just honour the work—they honoured the spirit behind it. I thank her for that moment. In her sincerity, she allowed me to breathe and honour myself. She gifted me the self-recognition to believe I deserved that moment in the throne room.

It felt as if Brigid was right there beside me, reminding me that leadership is about grace. It means showing up, again and again, with love and compassion, even when no one is watching. It's about tending the flame quietly and faithfully, until one day, someone sees it and says, *Thank you.*

That day, I didn't banish the imposter voice. I acknowledged it and leaned in, gently. I let it teach me that doubt doesn't mean you don't belong. It means you care deeply. It means you're still growing. It means you're human.

- What part of you still questions whether you belong, even when you've already arrived?
- Where have you mistaken humility for invisibility, and how might you honour your quiet contributions more fully?
- What story have you told yourself about worthiness, and what truth is ready to be rewritten?
- Where in your leadership do you still seek permission, and how might you offer that permission to yourself?
- What part of your journey — once seen as a weakness — is now asking to be reclaimed as wisdom?

Imposter Syndrome vs. Doubt

I am often asked if there is a difference between imposter syndrome and doubt. There is a subtle but important difference.

Imposter syndrome is rooted in identity, a shadowed belief that we are not enough. It whispers that we don't belong, even when we've earned our place. It often stems from early conditioning, systemic exclusion, or internalised narratives that tell us we must prove our worth.

Doubt, on the other hand, is often a sign of growth. It arises when we're stretching into new terrain, when our values are being tested, or when something within us is asking for deeper alignment. Doubt doesn't question our worth; it questions our readiness, our direction, our truth.

Brigid walks with us through both. She doesn't silence the imposter voice; she listens to it, gently. She doesn't banish doubt, she tends it like a flame, knowing it can illuminate what matters most.

When we meet imposter syndrome with compassion, we begin to reclaim the parts of ourselves we've disowned. When we meet doubt with curiosity, we begin to lead from the soul.

Both are invitations: one asks us to **heal**; the other, to **deepen**. Doubt, when held with tenderness, becomes alchemical. It softens the ego, opens the heart, and invites us into deeper listening — to ourselves, to others, and to the spaces in between.

I often observe imposter syndrome among women I coach in leadership. For example, a highly successful senior director I worked with was nearing burnout. When I gently asked, 'What would it take for you to pause? To take some time for yourself?' She hesitated and quietly replied, 'When I'm confident enough to know I belong on the senior leadership team'.

That moment opened a doorway.

As we explored her story, what appeared was the strength of the imposter voice within. She had come from humble beginnings. She hadn't been privately educated. She was the first in her family to go to university. The only one to have worked her way into a senior leadership role. And despite all she had achieved, she carried a quiet belief that she didn't belong.

But as we sat with that shadow with gentle curiosity, something began to shift. She started to see that the very things she thought made her 'less than' were the roots of her strength. Her journey wasn't a weakness; it was her wisdom. Her ability to lead with empathy, to connect across difference, to hold space for others who felt unseen — all of it came from the soil of her lived experience.

When we reframed the imposter voice, not as a flaw, but as a signal, it became a sign that something in her was still longing to be acknowledged, honoured, and integrated. She began to see that her leadership didn't need to be shaped by comparison or performance; it could be shaped by presence. By truth. By the quiet power of her story.

Over time, this shift changed how she led. She stopped overworking to prove herself. She began to delegate more, trust her instincts, and speak with greater clarity and conviction. But perhaps most importantly, she started mentoring younger women in self-worth. She shared her story openly, and in doing so, gave others permission to honour theirs.

One day, she told me, 'I used to think I had to earn my place at the table. Now I know I built part of it'.

That's the power of shadow work in leadership. When we meet the parts of that we've hidden or judged, we don't just heal; we lead differently. We become more spacious, more grounded, more real. And in that realness, others find the courage to be real, too.

The biggest changes in our lives and in leadership happen when we face our shadow. When we learn to be curious and to respond with inner wisdom, rather than fear, we grow. It's about being present with whatever comes up when we hear that imposter voice inside.

Curiosity is the key to being a great leader in all areas of our lives. If we're not curious about ourselves and about other people, it's very difficult for us to build meaningful relationships. When we think inwardly and listen with compassion, we heal. I invite you not to be afraid of what you might reveal, because when we are most curious about ourselves, we open endless possibilities of knowing our values and what really drives us.

Curiosity unlocks the possibility of knowing who we need and what we need to put ourselves in a position of strength, so we can really know who we are. We put our best foot forward and honour the full beauty of ourselves.

What part of your story makes you feel you don't belong?

What if the path of your story was your greatest strength? How would you share this with others?

Self-compassion through Self-Care

Leading through shadow moments requires inner tending. For me, it begins with the body; grounding in breath, noticing where I hold tension, and offering a gentle nod to *little Zoë*, the younger self in me who sometimes still needs reassurance. I keep a photograph of myself with pigtails on my fridge. Every day, I look at her with love. Holding her in my mind helps me find self-compassion when those moments arise.

But there are days when self-compassion feels out of reach. When the inner flame flickers and I can't quite find the warmth within. On those days, I've learned to seek external sources of nurture — living experiences and exemplars of kindness that hold meaning for me. I call these **Beauty Flames.** They shine light into the shadowed places and help nourish the parts of me still learning to grow. **Beauty Flames** are the living symbols of love, safety, and remembrance that help illuminate and soften our inner shadows. They are not always grand gestures; often, they are small, sacred moments or objects that carry emotional resonance.

Some of the Beauty Flames I return to:

- I visualise sitting on my mum's knee, placing my hand on my heart, and letting her softness and kindness flow in.
- I carry a photo of my daughter at four years old, walking on the beach with my dad. When I feel stuck, I look at it and remember the love I'd forgotten.

- I imagine a conversation with little Zoë and visualise giving her a warm hug
- Wearing my necklace from India that reminds me of my dad being by my side

Think of a moment, image, or object that brings you back to love—something that reminds you of who you are beneath the ache. What do you return to when you feel lost or disconnected?

Examples of Beauty Flames:

- A photo of a loved one that evokes tenderness.
- A scent that reminds you of home or safety.
- A line from a poem or song that speaks to your soul.
- A ritual—lighting a candle, walking in nature, journaling.
- A memory of being held, seen, or loved.
- A piece of jewellery or fabric that carries ancestral or emotional meaning.
- A pet's unconditional presence.
- A book or quote that always brings clarity.

PRACTICE **Creating a 'Beauty Flame List'**

♥ Create a **'Beauty Flame List'**—a personal inventory of the things that help you return to yourself. Keep it somewhere visible. When the shadow rises, choose one flame and let it guide you gently back to love.

Letting in Joy: The Light That Rises

Shadow work is not only about sorrow. It's also about noticing the joy that flickers through the cracks. These are the moments that surprise us, soften us, and remind us we are still alive, still growing.

My mother, who now lives with dementia, spent much of her life resisting indulgence. Cake was always something to be politely declined. But recently, I found out that she had been hiding slices in her room. It was a quiet act of rebellion, a sweet secret. I smiled, not for the cake itself, but for the happiness it revealed. Some part of her still seeks out delight, savouring the simple pleasure of a jam doughnut. She is still very much here, quietly creating her own moments of joy.

And then there's Holly—a young woman I coach. At 23, she has walked through shadows most would never imagine. She has faced poverty, loss, the ache of an absent mother, and the complexity of an alcoholic father. And yet, she rises.

One day, she came to me, giddy with excitement, holding her first pen ink drawing of St Winefred's Well. She had labelled it simply: *I rise*. Her joy was palpable. It was a beautiful act of creating. She was claiming space, saying, 'I am here'.

These moments—the hidden cake, the ink-stained fingers—are beauty flames. They illuminate the path through shadow. They show us that joy and pain are connected, and that beauty is found not just in healing, but also in the quiet acts of courage within us.

Leadership is shaped in the quiet, personal moments where we choose joy despite the ache. When we allow ourselves and others to rise from the shadow with creativity, softness, and delight, we lead differently. We lead with soul.

A couple of weeks ago, I was asked at a leadership conference:

> ***'What are your boundaries when it comes to creating a culture of heart-led leadership'?***

I paused, smiled, and said, to a few gasps in the room:

> ***'I don't do knob-heads'.***

It landed. Not just because it was unexpected, but because it was true. It created laughs and smiles.

I explained that leading from ego means leading from unexamined shadow—fear, shame, guilt, anger. We become reactive, defensive, disconnected. We forget that leadership is not about control; it's about connection.

I smile while writing this, thinking, *I have knob-head moments, too.*

I know when I'm in one. Like when I snapped at a colleague for not replying to an email—only to realise later that I'd never actually sent it. I'd drafted it, saved it, and moved on.

Cue the red face, the awkward apology, and the deep breath.

I could have spiralled into shame. Instead, I laughed. I owned it. I found my way back to joy.

Because joy is a compass.

It reminds me of who I am beneath the ego.

It helps me lead from love, not fear.

And it teaches me that even in our most ridiculous moments, we are still becoming.

REFLECTION Leading with Lightness

- When was the last time you caught yourself in a 'knob-head moment'? What did it reveal about your shadow?
- How do you respond when ego takes the lead—with shame, defensiveness, or humour?
- What helps you return to joy, to presence, to soul?
- How might laughter be a form of leadership—a way of softening, connecting, and becoming?

The Way Back to Joy

'I felt the edge
of my own sharpness —
a moment too quick,
too certain,
too loud.
The shadow rose,
as a mirror.
I paused.
Laughed.
Softened.
And in that breath,
joy returned
as a remembering'.

—Zoë

Tending the Flame of Leadership

As leaders, and parents, we're not only responsible for holding space for ourselves — but also for others.

When a team or family member is struggling, our first reaction is often to fix, manage, or rescue. But meaningful, lasting leadership invites us to take a different stance:

- Be the coach, not the controller.
- Ask more questions than you answer. Be Curious!
- Create space for experimentation — and failure.

Failure, when framed wisely, becomes a pathway to innovation and resilience. When leaders model vulnerability, it gives teams permission to be real, to take risks, and to grow.

I've seen this unfold in real time. One senior leader I coached was leading a team through intense change. She was competent, respected, and deeply committed — but carried a quiet fear that if she showed uncertainty, she'd lose credibility. Her instinct was to protect her team by absorbing the pressure herself, keeping things 'together' even as she fell apart inside.

Through our sessions, she began to explore her own shadow — the part of her that equated vulnerability with weakness. She realised that her silence wasn't protecting her team; it was isolating them. By naming her own doubts and sharing her process, she created space for others to do the same. Her team began to speak more openly, collaborate more creatively, and support one another more deeply.

She didn't lose authority. She gained trust.

This is the quiet strength of heart-led leadership: caring for the spark within ourselves and for others.

Brigid teaches us that tending the flame is not only a personal act; it is a communal one.

To lead is to carry the flame to illuminate. To walk beside others in their shadow moments with presence.

- Where in your leadership have you tried to fix, when what was needed was to witness?
- What part of you feels uncomfortable with another's vulnerability, and what might that reveal about your own?
- How can you hold space for others without losing yourself?
- What does it mean to lead with grace, even when you don't have certainty?
- What flame are you quietly and faithfully tending that might help someone else find their way?

The Quiet Power of Becoming

'To lead with courage
is to walk with both light and shadow.
To honour our stories — the ache and the grace —
is to lead from soul.
To lead from presence by letting perfection go.
From tending the flame, even when the night is long.
From listening inward, even when the voice wavers.
This is the path of shadow-aware leadership.
This is the quiet power of becoming'.

— *Zoë*

Brigid, Keeper of the Flame

'Brigid,
Keeper of the quiet flame,
walk with me through the shadowed halls of doubt.
Bless the dark as I walk.
Let your light fall gently
on the questions I carry,
on the places I fear to tread,
on the voice within that trembles,
yet longs to speak.
Teach me that doubt is an open doorway.
A soft threshold where wisdom waits,
where courage is kindled,
and truth begins to rise.
May I lead from self-love;
and from the raw, radiant edge
of growing'.

—Zoë

Lean into the Shadows

Draw from the well; even in darkness,
the water holds light.

5

Build Your Fire

Tine*

* **tine** (pronounced: *TIN-eh*) — Irish word for 'fire'. It appears throughout classical and modern Irish and is the primary term used for everything from a small hearth-fire to a large blaze. In the major Irish dictionary, *Foclóir Gaeilge–Béarla, tine* is defined simply as '**fire**' (e.g., *tine ghuail* 'coal fire,' *tine champa* 'campfire').

Build your fire

Tend the flame with courage.

Leadership is not without challenge.

Resilience rises in adversity. Begin even before you are ready. Have the courage to keep going and find the strength to stand by your values.

Love yourself deeply—every single day.

This invitation invites you to build a flame that endures, even in the storm.

Building the Fire

'I did not begin with certainty —
only grief,
a handmade heart,
and the ache of wanting to help.
Reality was raw,
but I met it with open hands.
I believed the spark mattered,
even when the path was unclear.
A voice on the radio,
a nurse with a story,
a kindness ambassador with a smile —
each moment lit the way.
Improvisation became grace.
No grand plan,
just small steps,
a flint struck in faith.
And slowly,
the fire grew —
shared, tended, alive'.

—Zoë

Karen - Carrier of the Flame

Opening Reflection – In Memory of Karen

• • • • •

I had begun writing this invitation with Karen in mind—one of my dearest friends, a woman whose life embodied resilience, grace, and soul-led leadership. I had planned to place her story gently within the centre of this chapter, to honour her as a modern-day Bridget carrying the spirit of Brigid's flame: a woman who faced life's adversities with fierce courage and built a career rooted in service, compassion, and love.

But seven days ago, without warning, Karen passed peacefully in her sleep.

Now I write this opening reflection in her memory. To honour one of the most beautiful women I have known, inside and out. Karen practised love in action every day. She lived with courage and tended her flame with heart and passion. She built a fire so fierce yet gentle that her legacy will live on in every woman she mentored, befriended, and led.

Karen carried three distinct qualities that shaped her resilience in both life and leadership.

First, she held a steely, honest acceptance of reality—the joy, the mundane, and the darkness of extreme difficulty. She met life's edges with open eyes and a grounded heart. She was unafraid of life's struggles, disappointments, and losses.

Second, she held a profound belief that life had meaning and purpose. Her values were unwavering: kindness, compassion, service, and love. She lived them in every conversation, every decision, every small and silent act of care.

And third, she cultivated joy. Even in sorrow, Karen found ways to laugh, to celebrate, to lift others. Her joy was rooted in the full beauty of her honest presence. It was the kind of joy that comes from knowing who you are and choosing to live with integrity and grace. Karen would often say, 'I am gorgeous and I choose moi!' She loved herself, she loved others, and she loved life.

Karen was a flame-keeper. A soul-tender. A Bridget.

Her light remains in the spaces she shaped, the lives she touched, and the love she gave so freely. This chapter is for her — and for every woman who leads with the heart, who walks through fire and still chooses love.

Karen — you are the light and love that forever remain in my heart.

Karen's Fire

Karen's flame was ignited by adversity and hardship. As a young teenager, she found herself homeless — sleeping rough on the streets of Manchester city centre. From those early days of survival, she travelled to London, where life continued to unfold in unexpected ways. She gave birth to a child she hadn't known she was carrying, discovering her pregnancy only days before the birth. She worked in marketing and printing, then found her way into the corporate world, where she built a long and distinguished career at Bank of America.

There, she trained tirelessly, taking every qualification offered, never once assuming she didn't belong. By the time she retired at fifty, Karen had risen to become one of the highest-performing board directors of people at Bank of America. Her remarkable achievements were not born from privilege or ease; they were carved from hard work, grace, and a refusal to be defined by circumstance.

In the many late-night conversations we shared, I was struck by her unwavering capacity to accept the realities of her life. She didn't sugarcoat her story. She met it head-on. She faced life with honesty, humility, and a quiet strength that allowed her to act in ways that enabled survival, endurance, and ultimately, transformation. Karen trained herself to survive before the fact. She was prepared, not hardened. She was honest, not bitter. She loved, forgave, and gifted compassion to all those around her.

Her acceptance of reality was intimately tied to her capacity to find meaning in suffering. At every difficult turn, she crafted stories to understand it. She never tried to escape life's harsh realities. Her mantra was never 'Why me?' but always 'Why *not* me?' She often spoke of the incredible friends and colleagues who walked beside her, helped her carry the weight, and gave her life its deepest meaning.

Karen was a weaver and a bridge-builder. She enriched her tapestry with every thread of hardship and hope, always moving forward to a more expansive, soul-aligned future. She saw her role in life as one of service: to be the bright sunflower in someone else's day, to help others recognise their best qualities, and to bring laughter into the boardroom, the kitchen, and often a really cool wine bar!

She made do with whatever was at hand. Karen bounced back from adversity time and again with an inventiveness that came from the heart. She had an uncanny ability to improvise a solution to any problem without obvious tools — listening inwardly, trusting her instincts, and finding ways to keep the fire burning. Her most powerful tool was her outlook on life: she chose positivity, and she practised gratitude even in the face of adversity. She knew when she was facing an 'it's a shitter moment' and chose to sparkle brightly anyway. She carried as much glitter in her heart as she did on her socks. She believed in the power of affirmation, committing her joys, triumphs, and moments of grace to the written word. Her 'Happy Friday' WhatsApp messages reminded all that life was full of sunlit moments, even in the rain.

For Karen, resilience was an innate reflex. A way of being. A way of understanding the world that was deeply engraved in her heart and soul.

REFLECTION

Karen's life teaches us that resilience exists in the present.

That leadership is about tending the precious flame, especially when the rains come and the wind howls. She showed us that joy can coexist with sorrow, and that meaning can be made from even the darkest threads.

- *Who in your life has tended your flame when it flickered?*
- *What tale of hardship might you weave into a thread of meaning?*
- *How might you honour your own fire—fierce, gentle, and enduring—today?*

A Poem for Karen

If Only I Could Be

'If only I could be
in your sunshine once more—
to feel again
the warmth of your radiance,
the quiet majesty
of a beauty unafraid to burn.
A Queen.
A roaring flame.

If only I could receive
a 'Happy Friday' once more,
and smile
at the sound of your voice,
that small joy
that lit the day from within.

No one sparkled like you—
head to toe in diamanté laughter,
your light
still moving through us
like a memory that refuses to dim.

Your love is not gone,
only changed.
It waits
in the hush between our words,
in the tears that fall
and the laughter that follows.

Sleep well, dear heart,
in peace,
in love.

For your soul lives on—
a soft breath
in the stillness,
a joy
woven through our grief.

You will always be part of
the light we turn towards —
the warmth that reminds us
how love never truly leaves'.

—Zoë

Building the Fire – Courage in Motion

Right at the start of *Silk Elephant,* when Karen sat beside me, we shared our desire to do something kind, something meaningful, amidst grief and global uncertainty.

What started as a handmade heart became a flame passed from hand to hand. And in that passing, I learned that courage is quiet, persistent, and deeply relational.

In the early days, I knew we needed to get our message heard. We were doing something powerful, something heart-led, but it was invisible. So, I reached out to BBC Radio and Granada TV. It was an impulsive, spontaneous decision, made in the moment, driven by my silent knowing. I had no idea what would come of it, and I certainly had no publicity strategy.

To my surprise, we were invited to be interviewed by Granada Reports, alongside Julia, a palliative care nurse from Salford who had received our handmade hearts onto her ward. That moment sparked others. From nowhere, hearts began arriving and conversations unfolded, culminating in an invitation to speak on BBC Radio Manchester. The momentum grew from the fire of human connection. My kitchen table became a sea of love hearts.

My dad used to say, 'You can't eat an elephant all at once'. That phrase stayed with me. It reminded me to take small steps, to stay present, and to trust the process. It's why the charity is called *Silk Elephant*—a nod to grace, to gentleness, and to the wisdom of slow, intentional steps. COVID and the charity helped me live that truth. Each day was a new climb. One step at a time.

And then came my starry sky moment.

Climbers describe the final stretch on Everest—the dead zone—where exhaustion threatens to overwhelm them. Just when they want to give up, someone reminds them to switch off their head torch. And there, above them, is the vast, breathtaking sky. That glimpse of beauty breathes life into the moment, giving them strength they didn't know they had.

Three months into *Silk Elephant*, I felt overwhelmed. I was grieving, working, being a mum, and trying to hold it all together. Then I met Lorraine and Jackie, our first Kindness Ambassadors. They brought the starry sky. Their presence reminded me why I started to share love through the connection of a simple handmade heart. From that moment, the network of Kindness Ambassadors grew. The fire was no longer mine alone. It was shared, tended, and alive.

Courage is often misunderstood. We see it as boldness, grand gestures, or fearlessness. The courage I've come to know through Karen, through grief, and through the quiet beginnings of *Silk Elephant*, is gentle and reverent. It rises from a deep love of oneself.

It is the courage to start before you feel ready.

To take a step when the ground feels uneven.

To reach out when you're not sure you'll be welcomed.

To keep going when the flame flickers.

To remember that starry nights will come.

Courage is the choice to move forward with love, even when fear, doubt, or uncertainty are present. It is the act of tending the fire again and again, especially when rain threatens to dampen the flames.

Karen taught me that courage can be gentle. That it can wear diamanté earrings and still hold the weight of the world. Courage is laughter in boardrooms and tears in kitchens. Courage can be both strong and tender—and still endure.

TENDING YOUR FLAME **Sitting with the Flicker**

You will need:

- A candle or small Flame.
- A quiet space.
- A journal or piece of paper.

Begin:

1. **Light your candle.**

   As the flame flickers, take a moment to honour the women who have tended your fire—mentors, friends, ancestors, or strangers whose kindness lit your way.

2. **Place your hand near the flame.**

   Feel its warmth. Whisper softly:

   'I honour the spark within me. I choose to nurture it with courage'.

3. **Sit and watch the flame.**

   Reflect on a time when you began before you felt ready. What helped you move forward? What sustained you?

4. **Write one sentence:**

   'My fire matters because...'

   Let the words rise from your heart, not your head.

5. **Close with gratitude.**

   Blow out the candle gently, knowing the flame lives on in you.

Brigid's Flame – Sacred Leadership

I often say leadership starts with a 'meow'— a tentative sound, a small voice. This is the spark before the fire: the threshold moment when we choose to start, even in our unpreparedness. The moment we say yes to the unknown.

Starting before we're ready means trusting the process of becoming. It is to acknowledge that we cannot think our way into leadership; we must live our way into it. It is to honour the sacredness of thresholds, those liminal spaces where the old is fading and the new is not yet fully born.

Brigid herself was born at dawn; that liminal space between night and day, goddess and saint, fire and water. She reminds us that beginnings are sacred, and that the spark really matters.

Leadership is a practice of sacred tending.

Modern Bridgets tend the spark that feels too small to matter, guarding the flame that could easily go out, choosing to step forward into dawn even when the night still lingers. The work is to feel willing, even though you don't feel ready. When we have courage, we can step forward without needing certainty.

In my experience, the truest mark of leadership is that others see we are willing to begin in the face of fear and doubt. It is important to role model that we don't always know exactly where the path will lead, and yet, as leaders, we take the first step anyway.

I talk to my two young adult sons (23 and 26) about this. When deciding to move forward in life, we don't need to feel confident before we take the first small step. I encourage them to act, to take that step, and let confidence grow through the process.

Whether it's young adults, emerging leaders, or close friends still discovering their true beauty, I notice how the need to feel ready, shapes the way they live and lead. It tells them to wait, to prepare, to be perfect. It creates hesitation and fear. The sad thing is that if they wait for all those things, they may never take the first step. They may never live the fullness of life, or lead with a full heart.

Leadership—whether as a parent, mentor, friend, or corporate leader—is shaped through action. We feel our way and find solutions as we go. In doing so, we build lived resilience. It enhances our sure-footedness with each step. This is real, living leadership from heart and soul. It allows for necessary change, brings joy, and helps others live and lead to their fullest potential.

Genuine leadership is born at thresholds. It flickers into being when we choose to nurture the spark, the flame, and step forward with honesty, vulnerability, and true humanity.

I invite you to cherish those humble moments of new beginnings. To trust even the smallest flame; that tiny flicker can then become a beacon.

'Leadership rises from the sacred act
of beginning—over and over again—
with a spark, a whisper, a flame tended in faith'.

—Zoë

* * *

'As you start to walk on the way,
the way appears'.

–Rumi

REFLECTION A Breath at the Threshold

- Take a moment now to pause.
- Close your eyes.
- Place your hand gently over your heart.
  - *What small spark within you is asking to be tended?*
  - *Where are you being called to begin—even before you feel ready?*
- Breathe in courage.
- Breathe out the myth of perfection.
- Let the fire roar.

Breaking the Myth – The Ready-Made Leader

There were many moments along my leadership journey when the myth of the ready-made leader shook my confidence. I looked at other powerful female leaders and sat in awe, believing they arrived at leadership with clarity, vision and gravitas.

Through many honest conversations over the years, I now know this is simply not the case. As my dad would say, 'It's as rare as rocking horse shit'. If you scratch beneath the surface of almost any genuine story of leadership, you'll find the vulnerability: hesitation, false starts, improvisation, and a step into uncertainty.

I spent some wonderful hours with the Irish beauty, Donna Scully—Owner/Director of Carpenters Group, a UK market leader in insurance and legal services. Donna rose from humble beginnings, leaving school at 16 and forging her path through hard work, grace, and relentless action. Her leadership is grounded in lived experience, and she now champions other women to build resilience through persistence.

In her conversation on the *100 Women in Insurance* podcast, Donna spoke candidly about the courage needed on the days when things go wrong. She reminded us that resilience is not about being unshaken — it's about showing up, learning, and continuing to act. She said, 'Continuous learning is essential for personal growth', and emphasised that identity is shaped through experience.

Her story is a living testament to the idea that identity is crafted through trial, error, and repetition. We don't wait to know ourselves before we act; we come to know ourselves because we act.

Donna speaks about the importance of embracing your true self in leadership and not conforming to societal expectations. She advocates for gender equality, social mobility, flexible work environments, mentorship across generations, and inclusive cultures where women are empowered to roar — even when their voices start with a meow.

Donna also lives and leads in service, running a homeless kitchen every Sunday and supporting countless charities. She helps others find the courage to take that first step.

Many of us were raised to believe that we must study, plan, rehearse, and strategise before taking the next step. Yet like anything that is ready-made, such actions often lack the imprint of heart and soul. Over-preparation can hold us back. Often, the more we prepare, the more we realise what we don't know. Sadly, by the time we feel 'ready', the moment may already have passed. Donna's story is a beautiful unfolding of a courageous beginning. Her success was shaped in motion, through persistence, presence, and the willingness to feel the fear and step forward anyway.

REFLECTION The Courage to Begin

- Take a breath,
  - *Where have you been waiting to feel ready?*
  - *What small act could you take today to shape your identity through action?*
  - *What truth within you is asking to be lived even when you don't know all the answers?*

Let Donna's story remind you:

- You do not need to be fully formed to lead.
- You only need to begin.
- To act with courage.
- To shape your flame in motion.

Kindling the Communal Flame

Karen's and Donna's fire lit the way for others, mentoring, guiding, and uplifting those around them with grace and loving action. Their leadership kindled sparks in others.

In the same way, Brigid's flame was communal, shared, passed from hand to hand. The women of Kildare did not wait for perfect conditions to light the fire—they lit it because the world needed warmth and hope that better times would come. Today, Brigidine nuns, Rita and Phil, are living firekeepers of that communal flame. From **Solas Bhríde,** in Kildare, and across the world, they are guardians of hope, of light, of eternal love in community.

So, too, did the women of my charity become guardians of hope. Every volunteer passed the light of handmade love through the network of Kindness Ambassadors. It was a shared tending. Leadership became a shared legacy, a flame passed hand to hand, heart to heart. When we feel collective warmth, we experience leadership of the soul.

Imagine a circle of women, each holding a candle. One lights the first flame, then turns to light the next, and the next, until every candle glows. Together, they form a circle of fire—a living symbol of shared light.

TENDING YOUR FLAME Compassionate Circle of Fire

- Take a moment to pause and create.
- Find a quiet space and a blank page.
- Draw your flame—as it feels.
- Let it be wild, gentle, flickering, bold, or barely there.
- Around it, sketch or write the names of those who have helped you tend it—mentors, friends, ancestors, strangers.
- Then, add one name or symbol for someone whose flame you are helping to grow.

This is your compassionate circle of fire.

Your leadership of the soul.

Values and Resilience – Tending the Flame Within

As I have learnt from the many resilient women I have walked alongside, resilience is about being deeply rooted by knowing what matters. When we know what matters most, we make a conscious choice to act from our deepest truth. We face doubt, challenge, and adversity with grounded reassurance. We walk on with grace.

Karen embodied this truth. Her life was challenging. She faced homelessness, unexpected motherhood, and the relentless climb through corporate systems that were not built for her. And yet, she rose because she was anchored. She knew herself deeply, and in doing so, her resilience became a way of being. Her flame was tended through values, presence, and living in love.

I have also seen this in women I coach who have shone through adversity and, time and time again, remained positive. They show an ongoing ability to reinvent, reimagine and move forward. I also saw this in the Kindness Ambassadors who worked tirelessly for my charity during COVID.

In all these modern Bridgets I have seen three qualities that shaped their leadership and their lives:

1. Steely, Honest Acceptance of Reality

Modern Bridgets meet life's edges with open eyes and grounded hearts. Like Karen, they accept the joy, the ordinariness of every day, and the darkness of extreme difficulty with clarity. This kind of acceptance says: *I see what is true, and I choose to respond with integrity.*

Resilience begins from this place. When we deny reality, we waste energy resisting what already is. But when we meet it honestly, we create space for transformation. We become capable of responding, not just reacting.

PRACTICE

- Write down one truth you've been avoiding.
- Ask: *What would it mean to meet this with open eyes and a grounded heart?*

2. Living with Meaning and Purpose

Karen's values were unwavering: kindness, open-heartedness, and love. She embodied them. In every conversation, every decision, every act of care, her values were present. They were the wood on her fire. They gave her strength, direction, and a steely focus on what mattered most.

Our values become our compass in turbulent times. They remind us of who we are and what we stand for. They help us make decisions that align with our soul, not just our survival.

PRACTICE

- Name your top three values.
- Reflect: *Where in your life are you honouring these? Where are you compromising them?*

3. Cultivating Joy

Karen—and all the women I've had the privilege to witness—have shown me this truth: even in the darkest moments, they find ways to laugh, to celebrate, to lift others.

Joy can often be overlooked in conversations about resilience. Yet it is essential. Joy keeps the flame alive. It is the warmth that sustains us. It is the reminder that even in sorrow, beauty still exists.

Often, women shortchange themselves on joy—believing

that unless they achieve or cross a certain goal, they haven't earned laughter or celebration. But joy is not a prize for resilience. It is part of the flame itself. Joy is what sustains us. It feeds our souls.

I see joy as a sacred act of receiving: a giggle, a song, a moment of beauty that reminds us we are still alive, still capable of wonder. Joy softens the edges of adversity and gives breath to the fire we tend. Joy is fuel.

Whilst preparing to be the celebrant at Karen's funeral, laughter and smiles carried me through.

The Amazon delivery of one hundred, one-metre-long sparklers to light up the sky.

The travel hair rollers were tucked gently into her coffin.

The wild Lady Gaga track was chosen for the remembrance photos.

And finally, my own choice of celebrant outfit—a bright pink velvet trouser suit with silver trainers.

Each choice honoured Karen. And, in its own way, honoured the family and me.

Letting in joy honours our full beauty and wholeness. We embrace the full spectrum of existence, sorrow and celebration, grief and grace. Allowing joy in means noticing what is good, even when life hits rock bottom. To giggle out loud, to wear pink velvet, to delight in the ordinary of travel hair rollers. To remember that joy is the light that helps us carry the struggle.

PRACTICE Letting in Joy

You will need:

- A quiet space
- A journal or piece of paper
- A small object or image that brings you joy

Begin:

- **Pause and breathe.**
- **Recall a moment of joy in adversity.** A time when laughter, beauty, or connection helped you keep going.
- **Hold that memory.** Let it remind you: joy is the light that helps you carry it.
- **Write one sentence:** *'Joy strengthens my resilience because...'*
- **Close with gratitude.** Whisper: *'I let joy in. I let it stay'.*

Let the flame of joy rise beside your courage.

Resilience as Sacred Tending

Brigid tended both fire and well—symbols of light and depth. In your own times of struggle, I invite you to do the same.

The fire represents our external leadership: the warmth we provide and the courage we demonstrate. The well embodies our internal life: the space for rest, reflection, and renewal. Leading with resilience means tending to both so we know when to act and when to be still. When to use our energy, and when to recharge. Resilience is honouring the rhythm of the flame—its flicker, its ember, its roar.

I see many women who persist until the fire goes out. In the ashes, they experience burnout, depression, and lack of motivation. I have sat on sofas with friends who have gone through full breakdowns. Sadly, they have nothing left to tend the flame or ignite a new spark. In pushing through, they forget to love themselves deeply.

I remember one of my earliest coaching sessions with Molly Harvey. She asked me, 'What is the one thing you would do radically differently to change your life'? Her question cut deep. My answer came without hesitation, 'To love myself the most, when I am the most lost'. Those words whispered to the deepest part of me.

It felt like a radical decree, and I have lived and led by it ever since.

So I step out with courage. When the winds rise, I tend the flame. I choose love. I honour my beauty. I return, again and again, to the well within.

Resilience is a profound love for yourself and an honouring of your soul.

* * *

'The wound is the place
where the Light enters you'.

—Rumi

SACRED TENDING **Building a Ritual**

1. Start with small, intentional acts.

- Choose one action today that reflects your values.
- Let it be quiet, meaningful, and aligned with who you are.

2. Surround yourself with your Anam Cara—Soul friends.

- Seek out those who see your spark and help shield it from the wind.
- Share your intention with someone who will hold it with care.

3. Honour your values—especially when challenged.

- When things get tough, return to what matters most.
- Ask: *What would kindness or compassion do here?*

4. Reflect, refine, recommit.

- Leadership is a living practice.
- Pause weekly to ask: *What's working? What needs tending?*

5. Let joy be part of your fire.

- Celebrate small wins.
- Find joy in the process, not just the outcome.

6. Let bravery be a verb.

- Take one brave step today, however small.

'We grow brave by doing brave things'. —Mary Daly

Keeper of the Flame

'Let me be a keeper of the flame:
a guardian of hope,
a weaver of warmth,
a woman who chooses love
even when the winds rise.

This is my vow:
to tend the spark.
to build the fire.
to become the light'.

—Zoë

Build Your Fire

'When the night feels long,
remember: the smallest spark
can become a beacon'.

6

Trust Your Silent Knowing

Intuigheacht*

* The Irish word for **intuition** is '**intuigtheacht**' (pronounced *in-tig-hyacht*). It comes from the root '**intuig**', meaning *to understand or perceive*, and the suffix '**-theacht**', which turns it into a noun — a kind of inner understanding or perception. It's a beautiful word that carries the sense of *felt knowing* — something grasped not through logic, but through deep, silent awareness.

Trust Your Silent Knowing

Practise Sacred Listening.

Brigid listened deeply—to the land,

to the people, to the soul.

This invitation calls us to do the same.

It is a return to intuition, to conscious

listening, and to the quiet wisdom within.

Silent knowing is the compass of

soul-led leadership. It asks us to pause,

to attune, and to trust the voice that speaks

without sound—the one that rises

from stillness and truth.

A Voice Calls

'A voice calls —
softly, patiently —
like a mother to her child.
She holds my presence close,
quietly attuning my heart's rhythm.
Each pulse
breathes life
into the words my heart whispers.
I rest in the moment —
to listen,
to sense,
to feel.
My soul walks ancient paths,
where every stone and silence
holds the whisper of wisdom'.

—Zoë

A Threshold

Opening Reflection – The Threshold of Silent Knowing

• • • • •

At the end of last summer, I stood at a threshold. It began in Ireland, where I spent quiet days listening with my whole being. The land spoke in whispers. I walked among ancient elder stones that hummed with memory and paddled barefoot in gentle waters that sang lullabies of grace. The landscape held me, spoke to me, and stirred something ancient within. Amidst this experience, a quiet inner shift began.

In that stillness, two voices rose within me.

One belonged to the Watcher. Vigilant, cautious, shaped by sorrow and survival, she feared the unknown, clung to the familiar, and guarded the wounds that once needed protection. This voice held the shadows.

The other was the Pilgrim—gentle, curious, quietly courageous. She longed to walk the path of the soul, to trust the unfolding, to step into the light. This voice held my full beauty.

The Pilgrim listened. The Watcher resisted.

During those late summer weeks, as I listened to both voices, I was searching for my next step of belonging, the next tending of the flame. I longed to return to community, as I had during COVID through Silk Elephant. I was ready to explore the next stage of service, as I walked into the autumn of life.

One of my Anam Cara—soul friends who walk beside me —is Molly Harvey, a true wisdom keeper: a woman who has walked the corporate landscape and lived soul-led leadership. She has spoken at the United Nations, coached senior leaders across the U.S., and shared her message in a TED Talk titled *The Corporate Soul Woman*.

I had the privilege of being coached by Molly, and during one of our sessions, I coined the phrase *Silent Knowing*. She taught me so much about intuition.

After returning from Ireland, I found myself debating what was next. I left Molly a voice note one afternoon. Her reply was simple: *'Are you scattered or focused right now'*?The question landed like truth. My silent knowing stepped in. In that moment, I knew. I would begin Inter Faith Ministry training that autumn. I would practise love in action in community. It was the natural next step, shaped by all that Silk Elephant had taught me.

Now, as I am writing, I am reflecting on who stepped over the threshold: the Watcher or the Pilgrim?

I honoured the Watcher's caution without letting it define me. I followed the Pilgrim's longing with discernment. The path of belonging is a becoming, and my path asked me to carry both hearts, both voices, both truths.

When I trusted my silent knowing, I felt the alignment. I remembered who I was.

Belonging to Ourselves First

To trust our silent knowing is to belong to ourselves first. It is to reclaim the inner voice of truth, and to trust intuition even when it contradicts the expectations around us.

Leadership in life, work, and community often calls us to act, decide, and lead with clarity. For women, intuition is sometimes overlooked or undervalued at work. Still, it offers real wisdom. Silent knowing is clear, steady, and trustworthy. When we honour it, we lead in alignment with ourselves. Our choices show our values, truth, and wholeness. Whether we're guiding teams, caring for families, or making change, becoming a leader means using discernment and courage. We are called to walk with both the Watcher and the Pilgrim, and to trust the voice within.

'When we learn to belong to ourselves,
we no longer betray our silent knowing
for the comfort of acceptance'.

—Zoë

This is especially important for women and minoritised leaders, who often navigate systems that reward fitting in over being clear. Trusting our silent knowing becomes a form of sacred resistance. For example, Brigid challenged patriarchal norms by claiming land with her cloak and creating spiritual sanctuaries that honoured women's wisdom.

Belonging to ourselves means leading from within. It's about trusting the silent knowing that comes from our values. This direction is rooted in authenticity. It helps us feel steady and in alignment. When leaders act from this place, they stay connected to what matters most.

This kind of alignment takes vulnerability and courage. We need to act from our silent knowing before outcomes are assured. Like Brigid midwifing both bodies and dreams into being, intuitive leadership asks us to trust what we cannot yet prove, but deeply sense. It is to take a leap of faith in what may unfold. To trust the process.

This is the heart of soul-led leadership: not just listening to our silent knowing but also paying attention to the quiet voice that says, *'Something's not right here'*, or *'This is the moment to speak'* and acting on it. When we belong to ourselves first, we lead with integrity and grace.

One way to tune into our intuition and listen to our silent knowing is to create space for the belly-brain!

Molly introduced me to the idea of the **belly brain,** the feeling in the gut that often knows before the mind can explain. Whether you call it the wisdom of the body, the gut-brain conversation, or just a deep inner sense, many leaders recognise this gentle, trustworthy nudge.

In my coaching, I've watched women change how they lead as they begin to trust their embodied wisdom. They stop second-guessing themselves and waiting for permission. They begin to lead from inner alignment, where mind, heart, and belly brain work together. For me, this brings a sense of peace, a calm feeling that says, 'I know what I need to do'.

In coaching, I invite leaders to include the body in this discernment—to notice the belly brain, the quiet intelligence of the gut that signals ease or constriction. When the Watcher insists on an immediate answer, the body often says, '*Not yet*'. When the Pilgrim senses a true next step, there is usually a felt sense of steady rightness, even amidst uncertainty.

The Pause Practice

Intuition is a form of embodied wisdom. It is more than just a feeling. Neuroscience now confirms what ancient traditions have long known: the gut, or **belly brain,** is a centre of intelligence. It communicates with the mind, shaping our clarity and decisions.

When we say, *'trust your gut'*, we are recognising a real source of knowledge.

To step into this wisdom, we need to make space for it. Before your next decision or conversation, try this simple pause:

1. Sit comfortably. Put one hand on your belly and the other on your heart.
2. Take three slow breaths. Notice the rise and fall under your hand.
3. Ask yourself:
    a. *What truth is stirring in me right now?*
    b. *What feels quietly right, even if it is not fully formed yet?*
4. Notice any sensations such as warmth, ease, or tightening, and let them guide your next small step.

When leaders take this pause, they often stop second-guessing themselves and waiting for permission. They start to lead from alignment, where mind, heart, and belly brain work together.

Questioning Rationality with the Wisdom of Silent Knowing

Leadership has long been shaped by rationality; the belief that logic, strategy, and data are the only trustworthy guides. In many professional spaces, especially those dominated by masculine norms, intuition is dismissed as vague, emotional, or unreliable. For women leaders, this approach can be quietly corrosive. It asks us to ignore the wisdom that often guides us best. In doing so, it takes away our sense of belonging and disconnects us from ourselves.

When rational thinking starts to feel limiting, I think of Brigid, a figure known for her strength and calm. She encourages me to reconnect with myself and trust the quiet wisdom inside. Brigid listened to the land, to her soul, and to the quiet voice within. Her example teaches that true leadership goes beyond *what* we know and asks us to think about *how* we know.

We learn to lead by making plans, setting goals, and measuring results. We are encouraged to be decisive, clear, and confident. While these qualities matter, they are not everything. Leadership is a relationship with people, with purpose, and with uncertainty. It is more like tending a garden than caring for a plastic plant. Gardens need patience, presence, attention, and trust in growth that we cannot always see. The same is true for leadership that comes from the soul.

A rational leadership culture teaches us that if we prepare, analyse and plan enough, we will be ready. However, readiness creates a mirage. The more we prepare, the more we notice what we don't know. And by the time we feel 'ready', the moment has often passed.

Rational leadership urges us to override our intuition, to dismiss the gut feeling, the quiet nudge, the inner whisper that says, *'This isn't right',* or *'This is the way'.* It teaches us to mistrust our own knowing, and to defer to external validation.

Soul-led leadership begins in a different place. It begins in silence. In stillness. In the body. It begins with the courage to listen inwardly and to act from that place.

Silent knowing is about belonging—to yourself, to your values, to the path that feels quietly right.

When we listen to the belly-brain and belong to ourselves, silent knowing brings precise wisdom. It brings clarity that rises from alignment; the moment when something clicks, because it feels true in your bones.

I've experienced these many times in my leadership journey. When I founded *Silk Elephant* during COVID, I didn't start with a business plan. Instead, I felt called to respond with love. The idea came from the soul of silent knowing. It worked. It grew. It served.

More recently, my decision to start Inter Faith Ministry training was influenced by this same kind of knowing. After time in Ireland, listening to the land and to my own heart, I felt the call rise. Molly Harvey's question: *'Are you scattered or focused'?* helped me hear it. And once I did, I knew.

This is the wisdom of silent knowing. An inner whisper that helps us transform.

How do we integrate silent knowing into our daily lives and work?

We start by creating space. Silent knowing needs room to rise. That might mean beginning the day with silence, walking in nature, or journaling before a big decision. It might mean asking, *'What feels true'*? instead of just *'What's the plan'*?

I invite you to learn to recognise the voices within. The Watcher may urge caution. The Pilgrim might long to leap. Belonging to ourselves and listening inwardly help us discern which voice is speaking and which needs to lead.

In meetings, we listen to words and also to energy. In strategy sessions, what's purposeful as well as what is profitable. In moments of doubt, we return to the body — to breath, to heartbeat, to the quiet knowing that lives beneath the noise.

A good friend introduced me to Neville Goddard's book *Feeling is the Secret*, and its insight has shaped my confidence in silent knowing. Goddard writes that feeling is the creative force — as we feel, so we shall become. When we listen beneath the bustle and allow ourselves to feel what is quietly true, we begin to lead from alignment rather than performance. Silent knowing often speaks through feeling: a sense of ease, a quiet yes, a breath that says, '*This is the way*'. Rationality may demand proof, but intuition offers presence, and presence becomes the seed of transformation.

Recognising the Watcher and the Pilgrim

Two voices often rise within us:

- **The Watcher** is shaped by survival. She is cautious, protective, and alert to risk. In leadership, she says, '*Don't speak yet*', or '*Play it safe*'. She is not mistaken; she is guarding something tender.
- **The Pilgrim** is shaped by her soul. She is curious, courageous, and willing to venture into the unknown. She says, '*This matters, speak*', or '*You're ready, begin*'.

Trusting our silent knowing helps us discern which voice is speaking and which voice must lead. We can thank the Watcher for her care and still follow the Pilgrim with discernment.

Sacred Listening – Hearing What's Not Said

Sacred listening is a quiet counter-current to the expectation to perform and lead with certainty. It is active, attentive, and relational. It involves tuning into tone, energy, silence, and the spaces in between.

Listening Beneath the Words

In meetings, we often focus on what is spoken — the agenda, the strategy, the deadlines. Sacred listening invites us to look deeper and notice what is unspoken. What currents are moving below the surface? Are there subtle changes in someone's voice or pauses that reveal more than words? Does confidence carry a shadow of hesitation? Is the room's energy open and relaxed, or tight and contracted? These subtleties are signals. When we pay attention, we hear more than silence; we hear the truth beneath it.

I've worked with many women leaders who have a natural sensitivity to these subtle cues, and I've seen the strength and value this brings to their leadership and to their organisations' success. Sadly, so much of corporate culture conditions us to ignore these signals in favour of logic, data, and decisiveness. Sacred listening asks us to reclaim our sensitivity as a strength, rather than a weakness. There is room for both. We don't need to abandon reason; we need to integrate intuition alongside it, letting analysis and inner knowing work together to guide wise leadership.

Sacred listening encourages us to slow down, soften, and trust the silent knowing that resides within and around us.

• • •

During a coaching session, a female director shared her concern: her high-performing team appeared unusually subdued. Targets were being met, yet the energy felt flat. She worried some were overwhelmed. Together, we built confidence in her own intuition: that she was listening beneath the bustle and that it could not be ignored. At the next meeting, instead of pushing through the agenda, she paused and asked, *'How is everyone really doing'?* The energy in the room softened. One colleague admitted feeling exhausted and close to burnout. Another explained that team tensions were running high as everyone felt pushed to the limit. That honest moment opened a conversation about workload, wellbeing, and mutual support, leading to practical changes that restored morale and renewed energy. Sacred listening transformed performance metrics into a human connection.

Listening as a Form of Love

To listen is to love. It is to say, *'You matter. Your voice matters. Your truth matters'.* Sacred listening is a human skill that underpins soul-led leadership. It is how we foster belonging. It is how we honour the soul in ourselves and others.

In a world that often rushes, interrupts, and performs, sacred listening is a quiet rebellion. It is a return to what is real.

Pause and reflect

- Where in your leadership are you being invited to listen beneath the surface?
- What signals — tone, energy, silence — might you be overlooking?
- How could creating space for these truths transform your next conversation or decision?
- How can you listen with love?

Joy and Silent Knowing – The Unexpected Duo

When we talk about intuition, we often imagine solemn silence, deep breaths, and serious reflection. However, sometimes the clearest whisper of truth arrives wearing a smile. I don't see joy as frivolity. Joy can be a brilliant compass. It can signal alignment in ways that spreadsheets and business plans never will.

When was the last time you felt that giddiness, the kind that makes your heart soar? It's your inner knowing saying, *'This way, please'.* Joy is often the first clue that we are standing in the right place, even if logic has not yet caught up.

Leadership can hold laughter alongside strategy. How wonderful that clarity can coexist with delight.

My children know when I'm in that space of joy and clarity. They call me *'Tigger'*. In those moments, I bounce around as if I am seventeen again; full of energy, ideas, and a slightly alarming enthusiasm for life. Joy alters my posture, my pace, even my voice. It's as if my whole being says, *'Yes, this is it'.*

One of those Tigger moments came when I was pondering what to write as a budding author. I had been circling ideas for weeks, trying to be sensible, strategic, and—if I'm honest—a little impressive. Then, out of nowhere, the image appeared: a tiny mouse carrying a handmade heart. I practically skipped into the kitchen to tell my son, Joe, *'I'm going to write a children's book about a mouse'!* He looked at me as if I'd lost the plot, but I didn't care. I was grinning like a teenager with a secret.

One week later, I finished the book. Four weeks later, I had written a trilogy— *Whispers of the Earth*—telling the tale of a mouse, a mole, and a bee. Joy propelled and guided me. Silent knowing spoke through delight, and the result was a creative leap I could never have planned. It was a spark of joy that said, *'This way'.*

Neville Goddard's words echo here: *'Feeling is the secret'.* As we feel, so we become. Joy is a feeling worth trusting. It's about noticing where joy rises when you imagine the next step.

The Garden Wall – Cultivating Culture with Post-it Notes

At a culture conference I co-hosted, we transformed the room into a living garden with metaphor and imagination. On one wall, we created a giant garden mural, and each participant was invited to add Post-it notes shaped like leaves, flowers, raindrops, and, yes, even weeds.

We asked:

'What needs watering in your culture'?

'What's already blooming'?

'What seeds are you planting for the future'?

'What weeds need pulling out'?

Initially, people hesitated. But soon, the wall blossomed. Notes appeared with words like 'trust', 'belonging', 'radical candour', and 'less perfectionism'. Someone drew a watering can labelled 'laughter'. Another wrote, 'Let's compost the blame culture'.

By the end of the session, the wall had become a vibrant, living metaphor — a shared vision of what a thriving culture could look like. It was alive with colour, creativity, and collective wisdom.

That day reminded me that cultivating culture is about care. And joy, like sunlight, is vital. When we invite playfulness and metaphor into leadership, we gain roots.

That conference reminded me: when we allow ourselves to play, imagine, and feel, we unlock a deeper kind of knowing.

I invite you to ask yourself:

- Where does joy show up in my leadership or life?
- What makes me feel quietly alive?
- Could following that spark be wiser than forcing another plan?

Joy is a doorway, like a summer wisteria archway in full bloom. And when you walk through it, you might just find the silent knowing waiting on the other side, smiling.

PRACTICE **Letting in Joy as Guidance**

This practice helps you notice where joy guides you towards what feels quietly true.

1. Place a hand on your heart. Breathe slowly.
2. Ask: *Where does joy arise when I imagine the next step? What small act today feels quietly right?*
3. Write: '**Silent knowing speaks through joy when I...**' and, '**Today, I will follow that whisper by...**'

Take one small step.

The Gift of Not Knowing

Corporate culture often equates confidence with competence. Leaders are rewarded for having answers, not questions. Yet some of the most profound breakthroughs happen when we admit, *'I don't know—yet'.* There is a quiet truth: **not knowing can be good, too.** It can be a doorway.

Humility like this is an invitation. It creates space for collaboration, curiosity, and deeper listening. It allows the wisdom in the room—not just the wisdom at the top—to shape the way forward.

Not knowing can often be a **threshold**—the space between what was and what will be, where possibilities gestate. In Celtic tradition, thresholds are sacred. They are places of pause, of waiting, of listening. When we rush through them, we miss the wisdom they hold. When we honour them, a new kind of clarity becomes possible.

Why We Resist

Uncertainty challenges our sense of control. The Watcher wants guarantees; the Pilgrim trusts the unfolding. Creativity, innovation, and transformation rarely come from rigid certainty — they arise from openness.

I worked with a senior leader preparing an organisational restructure who wanted every detail locked before announcing the change. Some pieces weren't clear. Instead of forcing a premature plan, she chose transparency: *'Here's what we know, and here's what we don't—yet'.* Trust grew precisely where certainty was absent.

The Fertile Void

Psychologist Marion Woodman refers to the liminal season of uncertainty 'as the chrysalis', a period when little seems clear on the surface, but everything is quietly developing beneath. In nature, winter appears barren, yet beneath the soil, roots are deepening and seeds are preparing to sprout. Our lives reflect this rhythm. Not knowing is winter—a season of gestation before the spring of clarity.

This is the wisdom of **Imbolc**, Brigid's festival, celebrated at the turning of winter into spring. Imbolc marks the first stirrings beneath the frost: lambs in the womb, shoots emerging from the earth, and light returning after long darkness. Brigid, woman of fire and well, embodies this threshold—tending the flame of possibility while honouring the deep waters of patience. She teaches us that beginnings often rise unseen, and that waiting is not empty—it is alive with becoming.

Before founding *Silk Elephant* during the pandemic, I didn't know what was next. I only knew what felt true: a longing to respond with love in a time of fear. That longing became a seed. It grew because I allowed the pause—the not knowing—to do its work. No immaculate plan, just a faithful beginning. It worked. It grew. It served.

My decision to start Inter Faith Ministry came from this very place. After spending time in Ireland, listening to the land and to my own heart, I sensed a whisper. It wasn't loud. It wasn't logical. But it was unmistakably clear. Molly Harvey asked me, *'Are you scattered or focused'*? The question rang like a bell. In that moment, I recognised the alignment I had been circling. Not knowing had been the necessary threshold; listening made the doorway visible.

I am reminded of my walk in the Lake District with David Whyte, reflecting on his insight that sometimes we need the whole sky to help us recognise the single line already written within. Sometimes our world must be held by landscape and community before we can hear what our own heart has been saying all along.

PRACTICE **Practicing the Pause**

What if, instead of rushing to fill the gap, we honoured it? What if we saw not knowing as a teacher rather than a threat? Three ways to practise:

- **Name it.** Say, *'I don't know yet—and that's okay'.* Naming dissolves the panic and creates space for wiser choices.
- **Stay curious.** Ask, *'What might be emerging here'*? Curiosity moves us from performance to discovery.

- **Create space.** Walk in nature. Journal. Sit in silence without forcing answers. Invite the belly brain into the room: notice where your body says *yes*, *no*, or *not yet*.

PRACTICE **Micro-Practice: 3-3-3**

- **Three breaths:** One hand on heart, one on belly.
- **Three questions:** *What am I sensing? What matters now? What is the next smallest step?*
- **Three minutes:** Sit quietly without fixing anything. Allow the mind, heart, and gut to offer their quiet data.

Leaders are often surprised by what arises when they pause for even three minutes. A conversation that needs to happen. A simpler path. The courage to wait one more day.

PRACTICE **Tend the Flame of Knowing**

This practice encourages you to honour your inner flame while listening for the whisper of truth within.

You will need:

- A candle or small flame.
- A journal or piece of paper.
- A quiet space.

Begin:

- Light your candle. Let it represent the spark of inner knowing—the clarity that arises from stillness.
- Close your eyes and ask:
- *What am I being asked to listen to right now?*
- *Where is the Watcher speaking? Where is the Pilgrim inviting me forward?*

Reflect:

- Write one sentence:
- **'My silent knowing is sustained by...'**
- Then write another:
- **'I will honour this knowing by...'**

Gently blow out the candle, imagining the flame lingering in your breath and choices. Let this act remind you that tending your flame starts with listening.

Closing Invocation

May you listen for the voice
that speaks without sound.
May you honour the Watcher's care
and the Pilgrim's courage.
May you welcome the threshold,
bless the not knowing,
and trust the one clear line
already written inside you.

Trust Your Silent Knowing

Listen for the whisper beneath the noise;
it speaks the language of the soul.

7

Be Still

Ciúnas *

* The Irish word for **stillness** is '**ciúnas**' (pronounced *kyoo-nas*). It carries a beautiful depth — not just silence, but a kind of peaceful quiet, a gentle calm. It's often used in poetic and spiritual contexts to evoke a sense of inner stillness or serene presence.

Be Still—Return to Ciúnas

Value stillness as wisdom.

This final invitation is a call to pause.

To rest. To reflect. To create sacred gaps.

It is in the stillness that we hear the whisper

of the soul, the rhythm of the seasons,

and with attention to the world, we find

the truth of what matters most.

Stillness is the beauty of presence.

The Gift

'As women, we weave
a living tapestry;
each thread
binding us in quiet grace,
loving and giving,
planning, doing,
holding all we carry—
queens of action,
in perpetual motion,
woven into every moment.
But what if we stood still?

Paused in silence,
to breathe,
to listen,
to root in our own beauty,
and mother ourselves—
heart, body, soul.
In stillness,
we gift belonging,
a promise of rewilding,
renewing.

Like a spring bulb,
we flourish,
awakening colour and sweet scent.

As we embrace ritual,
we cultivate seeds of joy;
a summer meadow
bursting into bloom,
alive with the sun.

Each moment a flower,
nourished by the quiet of our care.

And when we return
to the stillness once more,
we remember:
in the pause,
we gift ourselves
both soil
and bloom,
ever becoming,
ever blooming,
a tapestry of love
woven through every breath’.

—***Zoë***

Silence is Essential

Opening Reflection – Honouring Stillness

Through grief, loss, disappointment, upheaval, and countless challenges, stillness has always brought me home to who I am. In those pauses, I rediscovered life's meaning and the quiet power of love. In stillness, I have found wisdom.

With time and experience, I have learned to value the importance of being still. As a mother, colleague, and friend, I have found that pausing often leads to moments of grace. In these quiet moments, my sense of presence deepens. Here, relationships breathe too.

I couldn't have written this final invitation without walking alongside the poet David Whyte. I shared this experience with a beautiful group of souls who travelled to the Lake District from all over the world. This photo I hold from the tour tells a story. As I sat there, I reached a peak of happiness. It was hard-earned and well-worn. This happiness only comes after walking through deep sadness, grief and loss.

The walk to that peak was tough. I moved in silence, reflecting as I struggled with the challenging terrain. At times, I had to stop and simply breathe. The landscape invited me to meet the shadows I had been carrying. The grief of losing my father, the ache of a long-term relationship ending, and the quiet courage it had taken to embrace new beginnings. As I sat on the summit, overlooking the valley below, I felt the stillness come alive. The silence cupped the pulse of my own breath. Everything became crystal clear. It was an intense yet tender moment of realisation. I felt the sacredness of stillness. I will forever treasure, value, and honour those moments in the pause, where we truly find belonging. Our deepest truths are spoken in the hush. That trek to that summit was a threshold; it offered a space between what was in my life and what I was becoming. It invited me into a place where I could finally see the divinity in stillness. It is the breath before the word. The pause that makes the next step possible. The grace of self-love that tenders the flame. We gift ourselves the quiet ground to bring courage and the bloom of clarity.

I invite you to honour stillness. It is the soil from which every invitation in this book grows. Think of it as the pause that nourishes, the breath that grounds us, the silence that speaks our truth. Feeding the soul begins with listening deeply. Weaving a tapestry begins by opening our eyes. Stepping into beauty starts with rooting ourselves in presence. Leaning into shadows asks us to create a gentle space for their truth. To trust our silent knowing, we turn to the quiet that offers wisdom. And in building our fire, the flame rises as we find strength in stillness. Every invitation in this book begins in a sacred, honest silence.

May you find your own peak. May you sit in its stillness. May you lead from its quiet strength.

* * *

'Silence is essential. We need silence,
just as much as we need air,
Just as much as plants need light.
If our minds are crowded with
word and thoughts, there is no space for us'.

—**Thich Nhat Hanh**

As I sat on the summit, overlooking the valley below,
I felt the stillness come alive.

Attention, Identity, and the Timeless

In leadership roles, we often focus on what people think; their worldviews and strongly held beliefs. Yet the beliefs we hold do not form our identity. Beliefs are, in many ways, the least interesting thing about us. They are a façade, a surface expression of something much deeper. When we lead only from belief, we risk narrowing our vision. We start from defensiveness and miss the joy of possibility.

Our humanity shines when we lead from the deeper self. We need to be curious about the parts of us that exist beneath belief. There is space for creativity and compassion when we find the stillness that allows us to see the person as a whole.

As I train to become an interfaith minister, I am learning an invaluable lesson about humanity's role in transformation. The beauty of transformation disappears when we try to convince others to believe what we believe. Instead, we need to be curious about the soul beneath belief. Connection happens when we truly honour the soul of another.

The sacred path for each of us begins by recognising that beneath every individual's story and voice lies a shared humanity. When there is space to love the individual in their wholeness, we can be fully present with them. This is leadership led by soul and taught by soul.

'If only our eyes saw souls instead of bodies,
how different our ideas of beauty would be.'

— Lauren Jauregui

When we discover what truly shapes how we are and those we lead, we are walking in the shoes of true leadership. Our full attention helps us clearly see the people we lead. We then bring this gift into all our relationships, home, and community. Our attention to the world around us deepens, as does ur relationship with ourselves. We become more open, and trust builds.

When we pay close attention, we expand our understanding of identity beyond the narrow confines of the ego. Our focus helps us see life in all its colour and raw beauty. We fully perceive the quiet signals beneath the surface. The currency of leadership is born from our attention. Trust blossoms, belonging takes root, and creativity is ignited.

Our deeper attention blossoms in stillness. In the quiet, we step into the timeless. We enter what poet David Whyte calls *'the untrammelled'*. He speaks of a space beyond urgency, where clarity emerges like light from shadow. The ordinary becomes the extraordinary. In the pause, the hidden becomes seen.

Time and the Language of Poetry

There are numerous deadlines, schedules, and demands for speed within corporate leadership. It has created a culture of measuring and managing time to the extent that we fear it.

For years as a lawyer, my days were divided into six-minute segments. My value was defined by how much of it I could bill. Time became currency. In the early days of leading my own business, I carried that rhythm and currency into the role. I filled every hour and every space. I was doing everything: drafting business plans, delivering projects, supporting my team, managing my diary and travelling from meeting to meeting. I was '**doing**' with no space for **'being'**. Thankfully, it was my late friend Karen who reminded me to pause.

One morning, she arrived with a packed lunch and had an honest conversation with me. She had noticed my rising levels of anxiety. She told me I needed to stop, to take stock. To step away from doing. That morning, I closed my laptop, left the office, put on my trainers, and went for a walk. Just walked. On my own, along the canal. It cleared my thoughts. It helped me breathe. In the pause, I saw what needed my attention.

From that day onwards, I walk at some point during the day. Usually with my beautiful, gentle, wire-haired Vizsla, Ella. I connect with nature, smell the air, and breathe.

Time no longer serves as currency for me. It has opened the door to space, to closer attention, and to being human. My leadership is now more open-hearted. Letting go of time as a mere transaction has led me to understand the wisdom of being still.

Poetry also reconnects me with that same wisdom. It brings me into an intimate space and honest dialogue with myself.

There is joy in embracing language and thought through writing poetry. The urgency of my busy life lessens. There are still moments when that urgency creeps in, especially while juggling a senior leadership role as CCO, caring for my family, and supporting my mum through the late stages of dementia. In those moments, I sometimes lose perspective, and what matters most loses its rhythm.

When I write, I sense Brigid's presence. I light a candle before I start, returning to her flame as a ritual of grounding. The flame reminds me that stillness is a return to wisdom, to soul, to the quiet truths that live beneath the noise. In Brigid's light, the urgency softens. The noise falls away. And the truth of things rises.

Turas D' Anam

'Often times
the step backward
lets the soul catch up
So that all our happy
hindsights harmonise
and wisdom builds.

Share your luck
Be miserly only
with misfortune.
In each seismic
shudder we learn
to trust the ground
again, humble again,
knowingly broken,
unrepentantly wounded,
proud to bare pain.

Laying claim to
the joy factory
of your body.

No more tariffs, or sanctions.
Wage cuts and glass ceilings.
Conventions, expenses paid, nor
lanyards or company position.

Often times,
this way you can live
in ways others simply
will not, develop sides
of you others simply
would not.

So feel the rhythm
beyond the beat.
Begin with a break,
and let your soul catch up'.

—Micheal Padraig O Suilleabhain

The Child Who Knew How to Listen

I wonder if you have ever believed in fairies?

There are moments when I am transported back to childhood. Like earlier this year when I stood in a doorway of a children's fairy house. I haven't felt that giddy in ages. I was reminded of my childhood fun of hiding in my wardrobe, hoping for Narnia, and long afternoons whispering to fairies in my garden. These memories remind me of the pure joy of children's imagination.

My imagination ran wild when I experienced the quiet joy of cycling down to the fields by the river, where I spoke to the fairies under the trees. I sat in wonder, watching the breeze move through the leaves and the sunlight drifting across the hills. I loved the landscape. It was like a prayer. It was a moment to truly see and feel the beauty of nature and to enjoy the innocence of a child's view of the world. As children, we invite mystery into our lives, and in doing so, we honour what is sacred.

Those moments of my childhood were meditative before I knew the word. How easily we embrace the gift of attention in our childhood. It is a gift I invite us all to reclaim.

As adults, we lose this gift. Wonder is diminished by being lost in efficiency, ambition, and striving. The soul remembers when we pause and sit in stillness. It calls us back through longing, beauty, and thresholds that have caused us pain.

Thresholds reconnect us with our truth, much like the moment after my father's death and the unravelling of my marriage. It was the pain of loss that became a threshold, stripping away the noise and opening a stark clarity: I needed to return to stillness and my relationship with the landscape.

In grief, I spent hours walking on the moors; my feet brushing through purple heather, and my hands gathering moss along the way. As I walked, deep insights surfaced. Through my surrender, I understood so much more. By simply 'being', rather than 'doing', I began to walk with childlike awe and gratitude.

In leadership, there are moments when we must summon the courage to pause during a difficult conversation. These, too, are thresholds. They demand our attention. As we bring our full presence into them, our soul leads.

'When we make space for wonder,
we see, hear and feel the beauty
in everything that touches our lives.
Through wonder,
our soul remembers the unity of love'.

—Zoë

As I write, I remember one of my favourite poems, *The Bell and the Blackbird,* written by David Whyte. He recited this poem during one of our early morning gatherings. I have thought about how the words speak to the tension at the heart of leadership: that invitation to turn inward in times of unease and the simultaneous call to turn outward. The poem invites us to reflect on the choices we have.

There is the inner voice, the quiet ground of reflection that co-exists with the external experiences of life that demand our deep attention. Both shape us. It is about knowing which one we need to listen to.

Write Your Way to Stillness

Start the day with five minutes of free writing. Allow your pen to move without judgment. Use your pen as a way of listening inwardly before the world begins to speak.

What is calling your attention today?

The Quiet Invitation

'There is a silence,
a hidden depth beneath the noise,
a stillness calling you home.
Our truth is found here,
at the threshold where questions breathe,
where the next step waits like a shy horizon.
To lead is to walk on the edge,
to trust the ground beneath your feet.
Do not rush the conversation.
Welcome the silence to speak;
gently and honestly'.

—Zoë

Active Stillness Crafting, Belonging & Healing

Many volunteers who crafted hearts for my charity found joy using their hands. Until then, I hadn't appreciated this myself. My creative outlet had always been writing. Many of the women who crafted for us were elderly or infirm. They were confined to their homes during lockdown, and their ability to contribute to life through creating was also limited by physical challenges.

One wonderful lady, Rhoda, wrote to me to share the profound joy she had found in making hearts for the charity. She was crippled with arthritis and had limited mobility. In her mid-80s, bright and funny, and full of spirit, she had not ventured far from her home for over two years.

She wrote:

'To feel the knitting needles in my hands once more and make hearts for your charity has given me purpose. The silence at home is not sad now. When I knit quietly, I remember I am a loving human. I know my hearts are a bit lopsided, but they are made with love. I hope you find a good home for them'.

I have sat with those words many times, feeling the deep humanity in them. I feel the gentle presence of Brigid. Her spirit brings women together to craft in the hearth of their homes.

'To bring the precious gift of hands transmuting love is to turn stillness into belonging'.

—Zoë

In the silence of crafting, Rhoda remembered love; love for others and love for herself. In the pause, in the quiet rhythm of her hands, that silence became a sanctuary. She was grounded back to her own humanity.

I was always thoughtful about where hearts were distributed, taking time to find the right home for each one. I later learned that Rhoda had lost all her close family through bereavement. I had established links with various bereavement charities and local support groups, and I wanted her gesture of love, her quiet whisper saying *you are not alone,* to be shared where it mattered most. Rhoda's hearts eventually found their way to a local bereavement group.

One day, the head of that group reached out to share a story.

A woman in her group had lost her husband to COVID. She received one of Rhoda's hearts and felt an unexpected sense of connection. She wanted to give something back. She wanted to feel purposeful when everything else felt broken. She couldn't knit, sew, or felt, but she loved origami. So, she began folding beautiful paper hearts for us. She built a bridge across the chasm of grief, a space that was so devastatingly desolate and lonely.

Months later, the group leader told me how transformative this had been. Crafting gave her a way through the darkest days. The rhythm of folding and shaping her hearts brought her peace and a settled mind. It was so powerful that the GP practice applied for funding to incorporate crafting into their bereavement programme. Crafting remains part of their support groups.

Crafting with hands creates purposeful silence. It is active stillness. Juggling grief, work, and family, these women found a way to pause and reconnect with love. Each heart they made was both an offering and a lifeline. That charity taught me that creativity can heal, even when words cannot.

The hearts were a profound act of healing and connection. They are living proof of what research affirms: working with hands is a healing art; a peaceful meditation that regulates emotions and restores self-compassion. Each hand that crafted a heart held its own powerful medicine. A medicine of reciprocal love.

Toko-pa Turner in *Belonging* articulates this beautifully. When we make something with our hands, we weave ourselves back into connection: a relationship with the material, with our own inner horizon, and with others who share in the making. During COVID, our handmade hearts were the antidote to loneliness and grief.

'What is handmade brings love into the home'.

— Inspired by the philosophy of William Morris

My home is filled with love and handmade hearts that greet every guest. From the red ceramic heart cemented onto my front step to the hearts hanging in the downstairs loo, they welcome me too as I potter about the house. Each one is a daily reminder of the medicine of reciprocal handmade love and the importance of staying connected to what matters most.

Among the hearts in my hall hangs a handwoven Brigid's cross, lovingly crafted in Kildare from straw gathered near Solas Bhríde. It is a symbol of protection and blessing, and as it rests in the energy of love from the hearts around it, it weaves the ancient with the modern. It brings a sense of stillness into my home.

For centuries, women have woven Brigid's crosses on Imbolc, the first day of February. It is a threshold day; a turning from the stillness of winter toward the renewal of spring. Weaving the cross is a quiet ritual of blessing, a way to invite light and renewal into the homes. In this simple act, women join hands across time.

Crafting as Active Stillness – Medicine for the Soul

How might you invite stillness into your life and home through crafting? Here are a few ideas:

Make hearts — from paper, felt, wool, or fabric. Choose your method: glue, sew, fold, or even draw. Each heart becomes a small gesture of love.

Create a fairy garden or tiny house — using treasures from your garden: twigs, moss, stones, shells. Let nature guide your imagination.

Nature Collage — Gather leaves, petals, and twigs to create art inspired by the seasons

Weave a Brigid's cross — Gather fresh strands of straw. Weave them into a four-armed cross, folding each strand over the next in a gentle rhythm of blessing

Letting in Joy – The Moss Beneath Our Feet

My kids have a running joke. Every time I walk through the door after a walk, they ask, *'How much moss have you collected this time'?* I no longer need to answer. I empty my pockets and share the joy of what I have gathered. I now have a large glass pitcher — a mini moss museum.

There is something deeply loving about how I gently place the varieties I've collected on my way. I feel the preciousness of its contents. It is a living memory. It holds the peace of stillness. It reminds me that when I notice the quiet miracles of nature, I feel most alive.

It was during long walks after Dad's passing that I began to collect moss. Whether walking on the moors with Ella, or huddling under woodland trees, I was drawn to touch the softness of moss. There is something about its gentle growth. Its presence beneath the shadows brings a memory of safety. When I sit in the quiet spaces where it grows, I sense Brigids's spirit. It reminds me of her green cloak, protecting and offering shelter.

There is a humility in its presence. It invites me into a place where the chaos of life cannot reach me. Like the voice of the soul, it flourishes in the quiet and shy corners of nature.

Moss invites us into the ancient, the quiet and the wonder of its endless shades of green. It grows in shadow yet comes alive in its simplicity. Once noticed, it whispers beneath our feet everywhere.

For me, moss embodies the interconnectedness of the cycle of life. It thrives in damp, in shadow, and in places others might avoid. Moss is the joy of the soft and slow. Moss is a whisper, and its gentleness invites loving transformation.

I see moss as a soft-spoken teacher. A reminder that joy lies in the gentle and the unnoticed. That stillness is full of life. I have found a profound connection comes from kneeling down, touching the earth, and bringing yourself into the safety of moss.

Moss teaches us that growth doesn't always look like movement. It invites us to listen more deeply, and to notice what others miss. Finding peace in stillness enables us to be grounded and to lead attentively. In doing so, we become like moss — resilient, responsive, and quietly alive in beauty around us.

Pausing in the joy of moss

Next time you walk in nature, pause and touch the moss.Maybe even kneel on the ground and notice how many shades of green you can see.

Ask: *What joy is growing quietly in me?*

The Whisper

'Transformation whispers,
a quiet voice of love,
unfolding in the tender spaces of our shyness.
Transformation blooms
in the peace of stillness,
deep in the tender roots of our compassion'.

—Zoë

Friendship in the Quiet

Friendship is about walking alongside those we love and listening. To become our own best friend, we need to walk in the same way with ourselves. We need to gift ourselves the peace of self-compassion. It is in the quiet conversation with myself that I can be honest and self-loving. I have had to sit with the rawness of everything I am, rather than what I expect myself to be. In stillness, we meet the parts of ourselves we've neglected, and we learn to listen.

Coaching gives me the privilege of walking alongside women and inviting them to walk in self-compassion. One question I often return to: *What would your best friend say to you in this moment?*

There is usually an immediate pause after the question. Raw emotion fills the space. It opens that quiet, yet gentle, conversation with themselves. They invite a loving voice. One that they haven't heard for years.

They realise that they have abandoned themselves. That they have been walking alone. They have silenced the voice of care that prevents them from resting. Instead, they march on. Through exhaustion. Through illness. They compare themselves with peers, friends, and colleagues, and, in doing so, keep striving for perfection. In losing self-friendship, they stop seeing their beauty.

In conversation with themselves as their best friend, they recognise their value, their achievements. This is the starting place for affirmation.

It is in the slow rhythm of writing that I find self-compassion. It has become my affirmation practice. As my eye traces the soft blue ink of my fountain pen across the page, I am invited to walk gently alongside myself. The silence of writing is a conversational prayer. It blesses me with what I didn't know I knew. It softly calls forth a loving voice within.

Without that loving voice, we lose our anchor. We risk not being aware of what matters most and not being able to trust our silent knowing. In its absence, we start to control, to become defensive and become overwhelmed with doubt. As we become more senior in our leadership roles, we stop setting healthy boundaries. We find it difficult to delegate. We micromanage because we fear letting go.

To lead from the soul requires us to love ourselves first, deeply and unconditionally. It is in the communion of being still, in the sacred gaps, that we find the care we need. In this place, we role-model self-compassion for others. We lead and live in joy and peace.

May you love yourself the most when you are lost. May you lead with a loving voice.

Writing—The Gift of Self-Friendship

Find your favourite pen or pencil and take five minutes today to write.

Place this question at the top of the page:

'If I were my own best friend, what would I say to myself right now?'

Let the words flow without judgment. Write as if you are speaking to someone you love deeply—with love, compassion and gentle encouragement. When you finish, underline one sentence that feels most true. Turn that sentence into an affirmation by starting with **'I am…'** or **'I choose….'**

Examples:

- I am worthy of rest.
- I choose to trust my own wisdom.
- I am enough, exactly as I am.

Read your affirmation aloud. Become your own best friend by repeating it daily.

Sacred Gaps

Last year, I coached an accomplished female leader. I listened as she described the rhythm of her days filled with meetings, tasks, action plans, emails, and lists. Always lists. She was doing everything. But when I gently asked, *'And when do you get time to rest and simply be'?* the question landed with a silence that said everything. She had no space in her life to pause, reflect or recharge. She was tired and running out of motivation. It had been months since she had spent a full day with her husband and children. Her laptop was open seven days a week.

She had lost the joy of what I call 'Sacred Gaps', intentional time in our lives when we pause. To simply be. She had no space to reflect or rejoice in daily triumphs. No time to acknowledge even major achievements.

The root of this was permission and compassion. The permission to gift herself the compassion she deserved. Whilst within a viscous cycle of work and repeat, she had no space to walk beside herself as her best friend. Over several sessions, we gently invited her best friend into the room.

From our conversations, her self-love nudged a beautiful shift. The gift of a sacred Saturday, a day devoted to family. No laptop. No mobile phone checking. Just the joyful presence of being mum and wife.

I weave sacred gaps into my week. Golden moments of wisdom, rest, and joy.

10 minutes to sit in the fresh air.

A 30-minute walk with my hairy ginger pooch.

Sneakily drawing a love heart in my daughter's notebook.

A 20-minute meditation to start the day.

Listening to what's happened with my kids at work.

I reconnect with myself and those I cherish. I remember what really matters in life.

And when I really want to listen deeply, I light a candle in Brigid's name. I remind myself to tend my flame with care.

We all need space to tend our flame, without burning out.

REFLECTION

- What sacred gaps will you take today?
- How will you make this a daily ritual?

'You should sit in nature
For 20 minutes a day
Unless you are busy
Then you should sit for an hour'.

—Zen Master

Voices of Wisdom

In May this year, I hosted my second women-in-leadership conference, *Heart-Led Leadership*. We brought the collective compassion of women into the room.

The energy was palpable. Women came together to share experiences of life and leadership, and to be vulnerable. Humanity was shared across many different voices. I can still feel the love of that unexpected moment when arms swayed to *'All You Need is Love'* by The Beatles, and the calm that followed in our closing five-minute meditation.

• • •

Among the voices that day was Suzanne, a brilliant law firm director, who spoke about stillness as wisdom. She shared openly about racing through life and her early legal career — always running. She talked about her drive to serve. To serve with fullness at heart. At times, this pushes her to the edge of overwhelm. It was the loss of a loved one that broke the cycle. Grief brought her into a compassionate conversation with herself. She found mindfulness. She began to pause.

Learning to meditate later in life taught her how to welcome stillness, listen and breathe. She opened the conversation. She was vulnerable. She brought other women into the safe conversation of how life can get too much. She gifted them the wisdom of stillness. Her go-to is a gratitude journal—a practice that grounds her, honours her, and sets her up for the day.

So many women in the room resonated deeply.

When women share stories in this way, we bring compassion and love into leadership.

It takes courage to share and honour the sacredness of the rhythm of your own soul.

REFLECTION

- What do you honour in the rhythm of your soul?
- How do you gift yourself sacred gaps—pauses that recharge and reconnect you?
- Even five minutes can change the rhythm of a day.
  I invite you to start there.

Tending the Flame with Pause

Imagine the hearth fire—a symbol of warmth, creativity, and life. If we keep throwing logs on without pause, the flames flare and then burn out. But when we stop, watch, and gently adjust, the fire steadies and glows.

Leadership is like that flame. In times of urgency, we often keep adding fuel—more meetings, more decisions, more action. Yet the flame needs tending, not constant feeding. Stillness is the breath that allows the fire to settle and burn bright. It is in the pause that clarity emerges, and in that clarity, we lead with wisdom rather than reaction.

Adding Fuel Without Pause

- **More meetings**—filling every gap in the calendar without space to think.
- **Constant emails and notifications**—reacting instead of reflecting.
- **Urgent tasks**—prioritising speed over measured thinking.
- **Overcommitment**—saying yes to everything without discernment.
- **Information overload**—consuming data without time to process.
- **Performance pressure**—pushing for results without pausing for renewal.
- **Perfectionism**—feeding the fire with unrealistic expectations.
- **Busyness as identity**—equating worth with constant activity.

Being Still—without movement

- Sitting by a window and watching the sun go down.
- Listening to the sound of rain without distraction.
- Breathing deeply for a few minutes, noticing each inhale and exhale.
- Sitting in nature—under a tree, by water—without a phone.
- Lighting a candle and simply observing the flame.
- Sitting in the darkness, gazing at the moon.

Being Still—with intentional joyful acts

- **Writing by hand**—journaling or affirmations with presence.
- **Knitting or crocheting**—repetitive, soothing movements.
- **Origami or paper folding**—focusing on precision and delicate beauty.
- **Gardening mindfully**—planting or tending with quiet attention.
- **Painting or sketching**—letting the soul speak as it comes.
- **Making hearts**—from felt, fabric, or paper as a gesture of love.
- **Clay work**—shaping simple forms with your hands.
- **Walking slowly in nature**—noticing textures, colours, and sounds.
- **Baking bread or a cake**—savouring the aroma from the oven as they bake.

Unexpected Forms of Stillness

Many women I coach are deeply committed to their physical health. They prefer movement—running, hiking, abseiling, more than practices like meditating, crafting, or writing. I remind them that stillness isn't always about sitting quietly. Movement can calm the mind and bring us fully into the moment.

Cold Water Dipping

Cold-water dipping is my go-to when I want to find presence

through the body. My first experience was in the icy waters of St Winefride's Well. I remember stepping out of the changing room into the cool downpour of rain, thinking, *What on earth am I doing?* I was grateful for my friend Tina's gentle encouragement. An avid cold-water dipper, she knew how to help me find the courage to plunge into the well and receive the moment as a sacred act of care for myself. Now this is a regular ritual of stillness.

From the instant warm flesh meets cold water, everything else falls away. The only thing that remains is the presence of your very being. It anchors you to the essence of life.

Those icy dips are healing moments.

Could you be brave enough to let the cold water welcome you and fully receive you?

Running

I am not a runner, and my kids will tell you that's a good thing. They take great joy in reminding me that I have the most ridiculous way of running! Apparently, it's embarrassing. So, my pink trainers remain for the boardroom only!

I admire those who can run with elegance. The women I coach, who regularly run in nature, describe the quietening of the mind it brings. They speak of the meditative rhythm and how it dissolves the noise of thought. When they run, the mind empties and they feel profoundly connected to themselves and the world around them.

REFLECTION

- What activity choice helps you be most present?
- What brings you into connection with the world?
- When did you last feel the healing power of stillness?

My little gift to you – Mini Meditation

If you have never meditated, why not try this 5-minute mini meditation? You may find it helpful to record your voice saying the words below.

Find a quiet place. Lie or sit comfortably and close your eyes.

1. Begin by noticing your breath.
2. Relax and slow your breathing to settle into a gentle rhythm.
3. As you breathe in, notice the rise of the abdomen and as you breathe out, notice the lowering of the abdomen.
4. Imagine a balloon inflating as you breathe in and deflating as you breathe out.
5. As you link with the rhythm of your breath, breathe in for three and breathe out for three, visualise that your body is gradually being surrounded with a golden light
6. You'll find yourself feeling calm and serene as you feel peace.
7. Now imagine a small, steady flame at the centre of your being—warm, golden, alive.
8. With each breath, see it glow brighter. Feel its gentle flames warm you.
9. As you exhale, let go of the lists, the deadlines, the voices that demand more. Picture them dissolving into the air, leaving space for stillness.

10. As you relax into the light which surrounds you and feel the warmth of the gentle flame within, simply allow yourself to be

11. Silently repeat:

    'I tend my flame with care. I lead from light'.

12. After five minutes, open your eyes.

Carry the warmth of that flame and the light around you into your day—into every conversation, every decision, every act of leadership.

* * *

'Be ground.
Be crumbles, so wildflowers
will come up where you are.
You've been stony for too many years.
Try something different.
Surrender'.

—Rumi

INVOCATION

Be Still

In the hush, the flame steadies.

In the pause, the well deepens.

Here, you are home.

Closing Thoughts

As I close this book, I hold the truth that I do not walk alone. That there is love and mystery greater than myself. A loving presence that moves quietly through the everyday moments of my days—the silence of the pause, the gentle conversations with my children, the dappled sunlight in the woods, the laughter amongst friends.

This book has been a sacred unfolding of my relationship with Brigid. I did not grow up with her, nor with a deep Irish heritage. For many years, I walked through life with little attention to the unseen, to the sacred. My awakening came unexpectedly—with a beginner's mind and an open heart. Less than two years ago, in a tiny chapel on the island of Ponza, Italy, I experienced a moment so profound it changed everything. It was as if light broke through, drawing me into a deep connection of mind, body, and soul—into the breath of a love beyond myself.

From that moment, I started listening. I began to feel. I started walking alongside a presence of grace that defies explanation. It has brought synchronicities—people, experiences, and places that seem guided by something far greater than chance.

One of those synchronicities was spending time with a beautiful Irish woman whose presence felt like a vessel of grace. Simply by being with her, I believe Brigid's essence moved through her in a quiet transmission of something sacred. That encounter became the bridge that led me to Ireland, to Solas

Bhríde in Kildare, to meet the Brigidine Sisters, Rita and Phil. In their presence, I recognised Brigid — not from books or stories told by others, but a felt knowing.

She led me to write this book. I have engaged in dialogue with her in my heart. I have listened to her whispers. And through these pages, I want to share this truth: Brigid walks with every woman who lives life with deep humanity. Her whispers also led me to tell the story of my charity — the women who wove a network of love across the world by crafting simple hearts, each made with love. These hearts are Brigid's flame made visible: a reminder that love always finds its way home.

I have written this book as an invitation to pause, and to encourage those who walk a corporate path, as I have, to listen deeply and sacredly. My intention is to bring the whisper of Bridget into spaces where she may not have been heard, to serve as a vessel of grace to those women who, like me, may not have listened so closely to the unseen and the sacred. Women who may not have walked with the ancient and unseen, but are quietly connected to the spirit of Brigid's flame — women who lead and live with a deep connection to love, willing to both give and receive through a belief in humanity.

Afterword

As I travelled through the pages of this book, Brigid's presence felt close beside me. Her flame cast a gentle light, revealing stories, reflections, and emotions just when I needed them most.

I believe there is a love beyond us that guides us. This love weaves together synchronicities of people, events, and quiet wonders of nature. You may call it God, Spirit, the Divine, the Creator, or just a quiet sense that something greater is with us.

I offer this story, this glimmer of grace, as an invitation to marvel at the mysterious ways love moves through our lives.

I had been searching for the original heart Katie gave me that day on Dad's cancer ward. That heart brought the quiet power of love into my life at just the right moment. When I moved home over a year ago, the heart went missing. I searched everywhere.

Then, on Friday, 31st October, as I sat in stillness, quietly remembering my late friend Karen, with the flicker of candle-light beside me, something nudged me to open the drawers in the lounge one more time. And there it was. Waiting. It brought me back to that silent moment when Katie handed it to me seven years ago. As I gathered it into my hand, I felt the overwhelming presence of love.

The poignancy of that date is not lost on me. Seven years ago, this was the week we were waiting for Dad's results; the genetic testing on the strain of his acute myeloid leukaemia. We had been waiting for them to come back from London. It felt like a lifetime. In the deep sorrow of that week, I took some time to travel to Warkworth, Northumberland, walking in stillness along wild beaches. Time to feel the bracing sea air on my face; time to remind myself of the preciousness of life itself. On the way home on the train, I wrote a poem for Dad.

Today, I have searched for the email exchange between us to once again bring myself close to his voice.

His reply on 20th October 2018, exactly as he wrote it.

> *Morning Zoë,*
>
> *Thank You made me cry I Love you too and all your Family. Had text from Elliot which was nice.*
>
> *All good here, having Breakfast and Mum is on way. Saw Paul last night he noticed your Car but missed you, seems ok.*
>
> *Have a nice weekend all of you,*
>
> *Love Dad x*

As I sit here, I am struck by the simplicity of his words. Ordinary conversations about breakfast, Mum on the way, and a missed hello from my brother. As my tears fall, they feel like a benediction; a blessing to remind us that love often hides in the simplest sentences, waiting for time to reveal its light. Perhaps this is how the divine moves: quietly, through the language of everyday life. I read my dad's words and feel eternity pressing close. It is the presence and unity of everlasting love.

I feel the poignancy of my father's love, in its simplest form, 'I love you too'. Perhaps Brigid has been whispering this all along: that love is never lost, only waiting to be found again in simple moments.

Zoë and her dad, David

Eleven days after Dad's email exchange, we learned that his AML was the most complex and incurable. This was 31st October—the day that Katie handed me the heart. Here we are, seven years later, on the exact date.

This is a miracle. A reminder that love always finds its way back to us.

Love is ever-present, even when we can't see it in plain sight. It lingers in drawers, in candlelight, in the quiet cadence of an email from years ago. It waits for us to notice, to pause, to listen. When we truly listen to the wonder of life and the world around us, we remember that nothing given in love is ever lost.

As I close this book, I hold the truth that I do not walk alone. That there is love and mystery greater than myself. For me, this is Brigid's Spirit, a loving presence that moves quietly through the everyday moments of my days. The silence of the pause, sipping a flat white, the gentle conversations with my children, the dappled sunlight in the woods, the laughter amongst friends.

Through this book, Brigid has sat beside me, guiding me to live among the Bridgets of today, and to honour women who walk with the light of Brigid's living flame.

In the ordinary and the miraculous, in hearts found and words remembered, I hear Brigid's whisper: love always finds its way home.

I have chosen the path of interfaith ministry in the knowledge that there is a love beyond us that walks with us. This love is yours to welcome and to name.

May you walk with the light. May you walk in love. May you lead with both.

Photo by Julie Harris

Love Survives

'And through the blood,
the cells that run
devastate our lives;
but strength we have
with love and hope through the memories we share.

Dare not think too far ahead,
but enjoy each day that comes;
for all those times cancer cannot steal,
even though it lingers.
Love survives and friendship grows;
every moment we treasure.
We love you, Dad, for what you are,
and together we shall face
whatever route life takes us'.

—Zoë Holland

October 2018

Acknowledgements

To my husband, **Paul** —thank you for giving me the courage to find my voice through poetry and writing. For the endless cups of Rooibos tea, and for placing that beautiful fountain pen in my hand—gifting me the quiet space where the first words could form. You believed in the voice before it was ready to be heard.

• • •

To my children, **Elliott, Joe,** and **Lorien**—thank you for your quiet encouragement, your gentle presence, and for being constant sources of inspiration. You are beautiful human beings, and it is an honour to walk this path alongside you.

• • •

To my dear friends and colleagues—thank you for holding space for this journey.

• • •

To **Molly Harvey** and **Christine Pedros**—thank you for the light of your inspiration and the deep well of insight you both so freely share.

• • •

To my late friend, **Karen Flavell**, for your listening ear and the late-night conversations that always seemed to arrive right on time. You remain with me in the stillness of my breath. You are the light I turn toward.

• • •

To **Tina Symes**, for your deep wisdom, truth and warmth of inner flame.

• • •

To **Mimi Lyddon-Hardie**, for welcoming all the spiritual parts of me without hesitation—and for making space for magic.

• • •

And finally, to my late father, **David**—thank you for teaching me resilience, for showing me the value of listening to my silent knowing, and for sharing so many years with the joy of laughter.

You remain in the spaces between the words, always.

Katie Weaver, whose handmade heart became the seed of Zoë's charity. Captured at my father's funeral in January 2020, this moment is a testament to how women support women in the softest, strongest ways—across ages, across stories, across seasons of the heart.

REFLECTION

When I think of Brigid

Faoi Bhrat Bhríde sinne go léir

May we be under Brigid's cloak/mantle

I think of a woman who crossed a major threshold in 5th century Ireland, carrying within her the wisdom gleaned from her Celtic past and the seeds of a slowly emerging future.

I think of her imbibing and embracing the Gospel story that gave new meaning, passion and purpose to her life as she allowed its message to seep into her heart and inform her relationships and actions.

I think of her blazing a trail for soul-filled female leadership, and of her immense courage in founding a double monastery for women and men in an overwhelmingly patriarchal and hierarchical society. She invited a hermit, named Conleth, to assist her in taking charge of the male community and early writings indicate that they ruled 'by means of a mutually happy alliance'.

I think of her extraordinary care of and outreach to the poor and oppressed people of that time. 'What is mine is theirs' is a saying attributed to her when a wealthy lady upbraided her when she gave away the apples she had gifted her to a family in need of food. A sense of compassionate love and justice impelled Brigid to share with those on the margins. Her hospitable heart and hearth were inclusive of all, with a special welcome for the stranger.

I think of how renowned she was as a peacemaker and of her listening presence when often called upon to mediate between rival factions to bring healing and reconciliation. In a legend she gives away her father's precious sword so that it could be bartered to feed a hungry family. A sword, a weapon of war in Brigid's hands, was transformed into a life- giving instrument. The world needs leaders with a Brigid vision, heart and spirit at this time.

I think of her as a woman of deep faith and contemplation who drew strength and energy from her constant awareness of the presence of God in everyone and everything, reminding us of the sacredness of all creation. She gently challenged St. Brendan for being too busy and invited him to mindful practice of the divine in his daily life. 'She prayed as she was wont to do' (Early life).

I think of Brigid and some symbols associated with her. Her cross, woven of rushes from the soil hangs in many homes across the globe as a protection against fire and disease. Her flame, having been relit in 1993 burns in Solas Bhríde as a beacon of hope, justice and peace for the world, and invites pilgrims/visitors to nourish and tend the divine spark within. Her wells continue to attract pilgrims to walk in her footsteps and care for planet Earth our common home.

I think of the legend of Brigid's cloak/mantle spreading miraculously over the Curragh Plain when she persistently sought land for her monastery. This legend awakens wonder and awe in those who reflect on it. Her cloak continues to spread metaphorically around the world today as people search for a spirituality that is inclusive of all creation. May we all be protected under the warmth of Brigid's cloak as we walk together to co-create a more caring, compassionate, equitable and sustainable world.

Sister Rita Minehan
6th January 2026

Beannachtaí

By Nóirín Ní Riain

Seacht mBeannacht ar Sheacht gCuireadh

Bia Anama

Iarrann an chéad chuireadh sa leabhar ceannródaíoch seo orainn, aire a thabhairt dár gcroí istigh ar dtús. Gráigh do chomharsa mar thú féin is ea teachtaireacht bhunúsach shlí na Críostaíochta a shiúil Bríd, an Bhean Naofa.

Fíodóireacht Shaol

Is íomhá arcaitipiciúil den duine an fhíodóireacht. Is féidir lenár saol a bheith ina thaipéis de dhínit mhór agus d'fhéinghrá. Go spreagfaidh an leabhar seo gach léitheoir chun snáitheanna an áthais agus an bhróin a tharraingt le chéile i bhfabraic a fheabhsaíonn an domhan. Is fíodóireacht leanúnach de shnáitheanna uathúla an tsaoil í an saol. Sin an chaoi a fuálaimid tomhas ár saoil. Go gcuirfidh léamh an leabhair seo snáithe muiníne, seasmhachta agus misnigh ort ag an am seo.

Áilleacht

Fadó, dúirt an fealsamh Confucius go bhfuil áilleacht i ngach rud ach nach féidir le gach duine í a fheiceáil. Is é cuspóir údar an leabhair radacaigh seo—Zoë Holland—go n-osclóidh a breathnuithe ar Brigit ár gcluasa agus ár súile chun áilleacht a fheiceáil i ngach gné den chine daonna agus i saol an nádúir thart orainn.

Tine

Go raibh tine Bhríde ina cuireadh agus ina gealltanas ar thurais nua muiníne agus saoirse ó eagla tríd an léamh. Mothaigh teas na heagna atá taobh thiar de gach focal, léite amach ós árd. Rath Bhríd ort anois, a léitheoir. Go mbeadh aithne agat anois ar áilleacht d'anama ar bhealach nach bhféadfaí a shamhlú go dtí léamh an Crafted by Heart.

Scáileanna

Go mbeadh an leabhar seo mar dhídean agus mar áit chun scáth a choinneáil ort le scíth a ligean ann ar feadh tamaill. Muinín as an méid a théann suas, a thagann anuas, díreach mar atá i mbréagán an chlóis súgartha—an chonaic. Is é an teachtaireacht anseo idir chlúdaigh na leabhar seo ná go rachaidh seo thart freisin.

Intuigheacht

Nuair a bhíonn eagla orainn agus scáth an dorchadais ag dalladh ár radhairc, go spreaga an leabhar seo sinn chun Dia a lorg agus a chuardach mar a rinne Bríd i solas gach maidin.

Ciúnas

Go réiteoidh na seacht gcéim seo chun maireachtáil agus ceannaireacht le grá ar an cosán duit, a léitheoir, agus tú ag cur an leabhair seo síos go séimh. Seo seacht gcéim go dtí an seachtú neamh do gach éinne a chuardaíonn nasc Diaga agus daonna. Is é an leabhar seo an cosán a bhí á lorg agat ar feadh do shaoil. Go raibh beannacht ar an mbronntanas seo. Amen.

Seven Blessings for Seven Invitations

Feed the Soul

The first invitation in this pioneering book asks us to care for our inner heart before all else. 'Love your neighbour as yourself' is the foundational message of the Christian path walked by Brigid, the Holy Woman.

• • •

May the memory and model of Brigit, Holy Woman and pre-Christian goddess, constantly be a reminder to follow the path of care of the soul, first and foremost. 'Love your neighbour as yourself' is the motto of Christianity which the Holy Brigit of the 5th century lived and breathed. May you, who hold this groundbreaking book, be inspired by its message to know the light of your soul and to come closer to your true potential and possibility in life.

Weave Your Tapestry

Weaving is an archetypal image of the human being. Our lives can become a tapestry of great dignity and self love.. May this book inspire every reader to draw together the threads of joy and sorrow into a fabric that enriches the world. Life itself is an ongoing weaving of the unique threads of our days. That is how we stitch the measure of our lives. May the reading of this book place within you, at this time, a thread of trust, resilience, and courage.

• • •

May these Brigidine wonders, so beautifully outlined here, be an inspiration to gather together the threads of your life, to weave them into a tapestry that you will gently offer to yourself in love and dignity, at this point of your life. *'You never let go of the thread'* is the advice here of the American poet, William Stafford.

The German philosopher, Arthur Schopenhauer further recommends turning the tapestry of your life around to view the reverse side with its knots and loose threads. This exercise, he held, is the work of the second half of life when we look back and see how all the strands of joy and sorrow live side by side to weave the miracle of your existence. As you read, you are completing your spirit's purpose to live life to the full. Read each word aloud to feel the surge of belonging that is your heart's desire.

Step Into Your Beauty

Long ago, the philosopher Confucius said that there is beauty in everything, but not everyone can see it.

The purpose of the author of this radical book — Zoë Holland — is that her reflections on Brigit will open our ears and our eyes to see beauty in every aspect of the human condition and in the life of the natural world around us.

• • •

The very sound of the Irish word — *áilleacht* — is pure sonic beauty in itself. Pronounced *Awe*-i — lacht, with the emphasis on Awe is accurate. A thing of beauty, a legend of beauty which is Brigit's story, is awesome, full of wonder and generosity of spirit. May this book unfold a new spirit of awe in you which opens the door to the truth of your being. John Keats in his final lines to the poem 'Ode to a Grecian Urn' says it all about how truth and beauty are simply identical twin sisters. *'Beauty is truth, truth beauty,—that is all ye need know on earth and all ye need to know'.*

Build Your Fire

May Brigid's fire be an invitation and a promise on a new journey of trust and freedom from fear through the act of reading. Feel the warmth of the wisdom that lies behind every word, spoken aloud. Brigid's blessing upon you now, dear reader.

May you come to know the beauty of your soul in a way unimaginable until reading *Crafted by Heart.*

• • •

'I went out to the hazel wood because a FIRE was in my head' wrote William Butler Yeats in his poem 'The Song of Wandering Aengus'. The same flame awoke Brigit, both goddess and saint, to the mystery of her being. May she arouse you, reader, to awaken and ignite that flame of symmetry in your life, to burn away any negativity that is eating away, corroding into your sacrament of life and to shed light in the darkness for you.

Lean Into Your Shadows

May this book be a shelter and a place of shade for you, somewhere you can rest for a while. Trust that what rises will also fall again, just like the simple seesaw in the playground. The message held between these covers is this: *this too shall pass.*

• • •

The Irish word—*scáth*—carries two deep meanings; one of shadow and the other of shelter. In other words, our shadow is our shelter; our shelter is our shadow. A careful reading of this book offers precisely a wisdom as to how to negotiate this see-saw of life. Sometimes the shadow side is up, sometimes, down. The essence of the rotational motion of this ancient Greek invention of the playground device is that either the shelter or the shadow side rises while the other descends.

Trust Your Silent Knowing

When fear is upon us and the shadow of darkness blinds our sight, may this book inspire us to seek and search for God, just as Brigid did in the light of every morning.

• • •

Brigit, goddess and holy woman, was a triple embodiment of healing, smithcraft and poetry. So, too, intuition, imagination and creativity is a triple code that opens the gift of freedom from a frozen life. Brigit also embodies this trinity of continuum—intuition, imagination and creativity. This trailblazing book, dedicated to her leadership qualities, is inviting every reader to halt at the threshold and seek the good way which quickens your own triple wonders of life within you. '*Stand at the crossroads and seek and ask what the good path is. Walk therein and find rest for your souls*'. —JEREMIAH CHAPTER 6.

Be Still

May these seven steps for living and leading with love smooth the path before you, dear reader, as you gently set this book down. These are seven steps to the seventh heaven for all who seek a Divine and human connection. This book is the path you have been searching for all your life. May there be a blessing upon this gift. Amen.

• • •

The mystics from all traditions knew and preached the value of silence. Meister Eckhart, from the twelfth century, believed that there was no surer path to the Divine except through silence. God is there in the silence before we know it and this seventh step to leadership is the stepping stone to seventh heaven. Trust, dear reader, in this new beginning. Do not be afraid and know that in and through the reading, you are held in the palm of Brigit's hand. . . .

Rev. Nóirín Ní Riain
6th January 2026

Nollaig na mBan 2026
*Women's Christmas 2026**

• • •

***Rev. Nóirín Ní Riain** is an interfaith Minister (One Spirit Interfaith Seminary), an internationally acclaimed spiritual singer, theologian, writer, musicologist, and Celtic Spirituality expert.*

* The Irish phrase for '**Women's Christmas**', is '**Nollaig na mBan**' (pronounced *null-ig-nuh-MAWN*) also known as *'Little Christmas'*. It's the traditional Irish celebration held on January 6, honouring women and giving them a day of rest and appreciation after the holidays.

About the Author

Photo by Julie Harris

ZOË HOLLAND MBE, is an executive leader, coach, writer, poet, speaker, and changemaker committed to living and leading with love. Throughout her career, Zoë has championed the power of purpose — first as a lawyer dedicated to using law for good, and later as a senior executive shaping organisations with integrity and heart.

Deeply committed to serving others, her charity work, particularly her own charity, Silk Elephant, earned her an MBE for services to the community in 2023.

Passionate about creating impact beyond the boardroom, Zoë founded **Silk Elephant** at the beginning of COVID, a charity that distributed 110,000 handmade hearts and other handmade gifts across the globe. This commitment to compassion runs through all she does — from her leadership philosophy to her writing.

Crafted by Heart: Living and Leading with Love is Zoë's first book. In her seven gentle invitations, she invites readers on a heartfelt journey of the transformative power of collective compassion and leading with love.

Thank You

Thank you to the many women who supported the charity. With special mention to my mum, Heather Nichols for endless packaging and writing thank you cards and my late friend, Karen Flavell, for helping with the charity administration.

Kindness Ambassadors

Helen Selwood
Kay Lee
Wendy Parker
Ros Hammond
Lorraine Waugh
Jackie Dean
Jo Deighton — *and her beautiful Gift of a Heart Poem*
Julie White

Creative Volunteers

Gwen Simmonds
Edith Webb
Shirli Walker
Sue Burden
Victoria Sharman
Rachel Glasgow
Christina Tuttle
Fran Topple
Trish Roberts
Karen Wroe
Sheila Hardingham
Linda Wells
Lisa Ireland
Jackie Lawson
Alison Cotterill
Patricia Anderson
Lini Veerapen
Val Killingworth
Carol Winter
Cathy Lines
Emma Bradley
Kath Tinsley-Knibbs
Christine Wheeldon
Judy Hamill
Cathy Graham
Bev Tobutt

Charlotte Hey
Jennifer Wilby
Julia Allan
Mags Goulther
Wendy Bixby
Liz Murphy
Glynis scales
Reiko Tazaki
Sue Burden
Jo Rutterford
Judy Pearson
Ann Grierson
Sue Weeks
Jan Lovegrove
Susan Harbord
Helen Malkin Willatt
Julia Allan
Marlene Lissett
Fiona Keady
Jane Ludlow
Linda Wells
Barbara Heath
Jenny Phillips
Glynis Scales
Helen Fitzpatrick
Joyce McEwan
Claire Musgrove
Janice Refalo
Melanie Clarke
Fran Topple
Debbie Thickett
Sally Galloway
Laura Southam
Kathy Shaw
Marlene Pollock
Caroline Langstone
Vander Strange
Jane Ludlow
Laura Watts
Mary McCrimmon
Elizabeth Branston
Gillian Robson
Cathy Havelock
Ruth Green
Janette Harper
Cassie Muir
Zoe Sidat
Jill Elizabeth
Melanie Clark
Fran Topple
Caroline Lowe
Lynne Rye
Fiona Lawley
Daxa Patel
And every other woman in the Silk Elephant Facebook Group.

Children Volunteers

Niamh and Aoife *(Mum Lisa Marie)*
Mont Eagle Primary School, London
Lorien Holland
Neve Marsden
James Marsden

Printed in Dunstable, United Kingdom

79098804R00147